THE A
AND SEDUCTION

A fun and informative book on handwriting and what it reveals about sexuality, taboos, inhibitions, feelings, compatibility and sensuality.

Well Mr Bushell, I see from your handwriting that you're fantastic in bed..

THE ABC OF SEX AND SEDUCTION

What handwriting reveals about sexuality, compatibility and sensuality

JENNY HALFON

Cartoons by Peter Utton

AQUARIAN

THE AQUARIAN PRESS
Wellingborough, Northamptonshire

First published 1986

British Library Cataloguing in Publication Data

Halfon, Jenny
The ABC of sex and seduction : what handwriting reveals about sexuality, compatibility and sensuality.
1. Sex (Psychology) 2. Graphology
I. Title

155.3 BF692

ISBN 0-85030-546-2

The Aquarian Press is part of the Thorsons Publishing Group

Printed and bound in Great Britain

DEDICATION

This book is dedicated to Sexual Norm's mummy, Tricia Simmonds, and my four marvellous men (?). Grateful thanks, too, to the late Jimmy (Clarence) Jones, Margaret Carlin, and especially to Mr Francis Hilliger for all his help and encouragement.

CONTENTS

Chapter 1

First Writes – The Secret Signals Hidden in Handwriting

This book is wicked, shocking, sneaky, revealing, cheeky, uncompromising and entirely below the belt. It will tell you all you ever wanted to know about your own sexual responses and how to become even more sensuous and seductive. It will also show you at a glance how you and your partners, bosses, friends, lovers, maiden aunts, neighbours and rivals perform and conform to the Sexual Norm.

The easiest, most direct and certain way of finding out this X-certificate information is by examining the secret clues contained in handwriting. It is also the safest, since it doesn't invite a smack on the nose, a divorce or similar unpleasant complications that other more intimate investigations may provoke.

The name of the game is script-tease; stripping down the script and squiggles of everyday writing to its vital parts. These shriek out a coded message about the personality of the character who wielded the pen. As an erotic indicator, handwriting is more reliable than psychological testing and cuts through image and ego to reveal the real nitty-gritty hidden beneath.

Everyone's handwriting is unique, yet the trends and traits can be categorized according to shapes, slants, loops and lines.

Our own cute and cuddly character, Sexual Norm, will guide you through the points to look for as a budding sex 'tec, spotting and identifying the various handwriting styles of the sexual and emotional all-sorts that make up this crazy world.

There is no mystic mumbo-jumbo about handwriting analysis. It is a precise science and is used in all walks of life today as an aid to understanding personality.

While its most intriguing use is in highlighting sexuality, handwriting analysis can reveal an array of facts about you, your health, taste, skills, fears, hobbies and happiness. Whether you express yourself in hieroglyphics, Chinese characters, Arabic script or any of the 3,000 languages currently in use worldwide, a trained handwriting analyst can work out exactly where you are at any given moment. Handwriting will tell everything worth knowing about you, except your inside leg measurement and the colour of your skin. Whether you cough up your lungs every morning, or if you are constipated; whether you have a sweet tooth, a sense of humour, a fear of heights or spiders – even whether you need to wear spectacles – will be indicated.

Handwriting will show if you are sensitive to sunlight, whether you are lean or muscly, fat or wobbly; lazy, indolent or busy, sporty, arrogant, proud, a born strategist or day-dreamer; if you are a fussy, picky eater or a hearty glutton, an intellectual or a dunce, a spiritual and high-minded aesthete or an earthy pleasure-seeker.

Also laid on the line is your mental state, showing if you are an optimistic, ambitious, positive, efficient go-getter or a negative, nervy, phobic, future-fearing and repressed no-hoper. Your imaginative, creative and visionary qualities are dazzlingly spotlighted, just as surely as your grasping, mean and nasty traits.

As such an effective and foolproof tool (so long as fools aren't messing with it) little wonder handwriting analysis has been taken up enthusiastically by industry. More and more job-hunters are invited to handwrite and not type their applications so that personnel officials can scrutinize the personality revealed by the pen. Employers who can afford to be even choosier than ever before in their selection of staff want to know if an applicant will get on well with colleagues and work harmoniously in a team; whether they would display creative flair, efficiency, persuasive salesmanship or indeed if they have the leadership potential of a boss, all of which is indicated by their handwriting.

Job hunters are invited to hand write and not type their applications so that personnel officials can scrutinize the personality revealed by the pen.

Companies who handle money or valuable goods need to know if a potential worker is honest and reliable and handwriting contains all the pointers they need to reassure themselves. It has even been known for banks and credit firms to run a quick and discreet script check over a client before lending sums that they might otherwise never see repaid again.

Handwriting sleuths have cleared up industrial whodunnits, from tracking down perpetrators of industrial espionage by comparing notes, to finding out who scribbled rude words and graffitti about the boss on lavatory walls. Criminality of all shades and styles, from theft, forgery and especially the identification of anonymous and poison pen letter writers relies on the basic principles of handwriting analysis.

Interpersonal relationships, too, become less hit-and-miss affairs if compatibility has been worked out in advance through comparing handwriting. Simple boy-meets-girl situations, marriage prospects, and the lasting and lusting power of lovers can be correctly gauged. In fact any close human contact can be checked for its potential success rating, from a housewife taking on a new au pair to a prospective mother-in-law seeking the low-down on her future son-in-law.

Before checking out the specific sexual secrets revealed by writing style, use the following simple analysis guidelines to help you identify key points.

Handwriting is divided into three zones:

1. The *upper zone* reveals the intellectual and spiritual qualities, including imagination and creativity.
2. The *middle zone* tells of your everyday approach to life, including attitudes to money and possessions and other people on a day-to-day basis. It shows how you interact with your fellow men and how you feel about yourself.
3. The *lower zone* reveals the X-rated information on sexual and physical make-up, the unconscious mind, erotic fantasies and basic drives and desires towards power, sex and money.

The slant of the writing also needs to be noted:

1. A *right-slanter* is a forward-thinking extrovert who

eagerly reaches out towards goals and faces the future in an optimistic way. Attitudes are modelled by the father's influence.

2. An *upright-slanter* is level-headed, cool, aloof, detached and has a totally objective, independent approach.
3. A *left-slanter* is a repressed, introverted, introspective person who hankers for the past and the might-have-beens. They are strongly tied to mother.
4. A *mixed-slanter* is an emotionally mixed-up character who can be fickle, unpredictable and unstable. With head and heart locked in fierce battle, the outlook of these pendulum people is erratic, swinging from one extreme to another. They dwell on the past, live for the present, and look to the future simultaneously.

The lay of the lines is also important.

1. *Soaring* lines show exuberance and elation.
2. *Rising* lines, like laugh lines in a face, denote a happy-go-lucky optimist.
3. *Level* lines below show level-headedness with a healthy regard for realism even to the point of rigidity.
4. *Drooping* lines show pessimism, gloominess, and disappointment.
5. *Collapsing* lines reveal melancholia, tiredness and chronic depression, like a downward-drooping mouth or crying face.
6. *Zig-zag* lines which jump up and down indicate a changeable approach including mixed-up morals.

Now check out your own erotic style with the help of Sexual Norm. If you discover any shocks or shortcomings, don't worry. Just as handwriting can reveal exactly what you are, warts and all, it can also be the key to a more satisfying and erotically rampant new chapter in your life, if that is what you really desire. Pen power will show you how ...

Chapter 2

Within Your Writes

Sexperts – The Best Bedmates

If the Olympic games included a section for the best sexual partner, they would be on the winners' rostrum. Everyone should enjoy at least one close encounter with a sexpert. They will set the standard by which you may judge perfection of performance for ever more.

Sexperts instinctively adapt their technique to bring

out the best in their bed partner, even a nervous novice. So skilful are they that any awkwardness, shyness or inhibition vanish. So powerful is their magic that even one lingering look lasering onto target can have a devastating effect.

They want to give as well as receive, synchronizing their movements and responses to match those of their lover. Even in the heat of passion, they are naturally confident and accomplished. Sexperts never need a

Everyone should enjoy at least one encounter with a sexpert.

rehearsal. Their memorable performances ensure many encores.

Their handwriting movements are just as finely tuned and balanced.

Sexperts have a normal right slant. The sizes of the three zones are fairly well balanced and their loops are completed and well rounded in the lower zones – particularly with the letter 'g'. In the middle zone, letters will be round and broad. Letters are partially connected and a few starting strokes will be shown here and there, plus extended end strokes.

Fumblers

Clumsy fumblers are like overgrown puppies who have not been properly house-trained. Although readily aroused, they cannot get their act together smoothly and easily, and often make a complete hash of it.

No matter how carefully they set the scene for seduction, their gauche awkwardness always produces some passion-killing pratfall that ruins the scene, from tripping over the cat on their way to the bed, to getting stuck in their eight-hour girdle.

Feeling awkward and clumsy in erotic scenarios is a hangover from childhood, when sexual exploration was rushed, flushed and guilt-ridden. As adults, calamity inevitably accompanies them on sexual adventures. Jammed zips, knotted laces, collapsing beds, cramps and smouldering pyjamas are among the hazards encountered.

Their timing is terrible, their movements jerky and lacking in rhythm, and their accident-prone performances all combine to ensure a crashing crescendo.

The more flustered Fumblers become, the more uncoordinated their performance. Self-consciousness, as inhibiting as a cold shower, follows, making their partner feel as miserable and uncomfortable as they do.

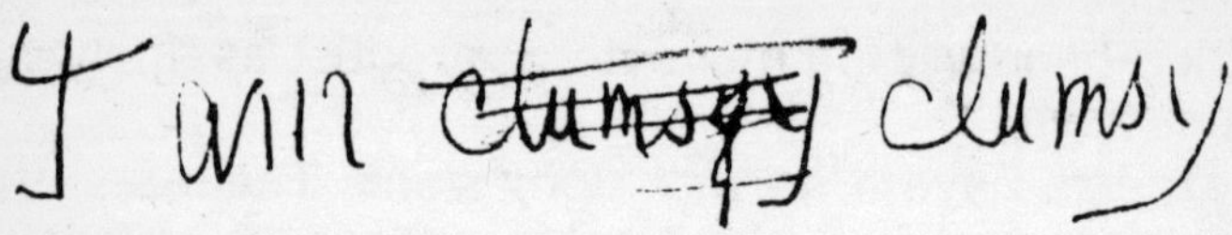

The Fumbler's script is upright or slants to the left. The writing looks narrow and uncoordinated, lacking in rhythm and of copybook style. The upper zone is smaller than the lower zone and left margins are irregular. Some letters are broken and lines mingle.

Pouncers

Thick-skinned and insensitive to the needs of others, opportunist Pouncers rarely consider waiting for the right time, place or partner to make their moves. Nothing stops them when their minds are focused on sex; as they believe in going for it speedily.

Niceties, like the willingness or otherwise of their victims, are of scant importance. They believe in grabbing the advantage and taking liberties before anyone else has time to react.

Patience never has been one of their virtues, and they can show considerable frustration if thwarted or aborted in their pushy, selfish and single-minded pursuit of satisfaction.

Male Pouncers grab the teenage typist behind the filing cabinet when the boss is out of the room or spring silently like a cat over the garden fence to leap on an unsuspecting topless sunbather. Female Pouncers barge into an unwary neighbour's house wearing nothing but a see-through nightie when his wife is out at bingo, or lure the milkman up the path for a clinch guaranteed to curdle his milkshake.

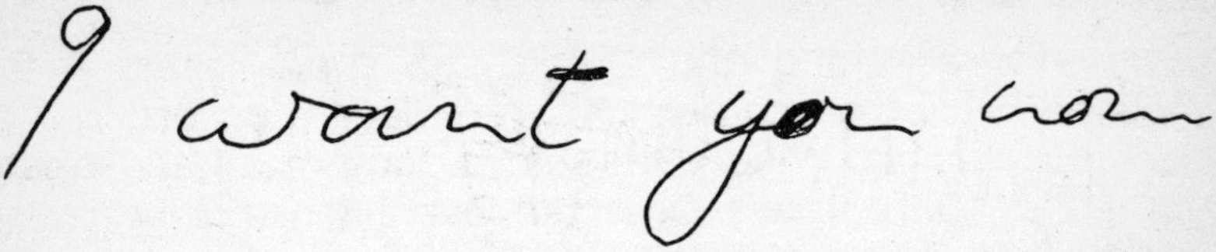

Pouncers show a marked rightward slant and long downstrokes. There is an uneven pattern to the height of letters. Letters are connected in a threadlike way. The size of letters varies from broad to narrow. Final letters of words become illegible.

Female Pouncers can curdle the milkman's milkshake.

The Naughty-Sporty Anytime-Anywhere Lovers

Game for anything and everything, these lovers with boundless energy and enthusiasm believe the word 'No' is just not cricket. Wide open spaces, long grass and fresh air act as aphrodisiacs. Deserted lovers' lanes or beaches, ill-lit shop doorways or alleyways, wooded bowers, campsite showers or any public location where they can snatch or swop secret intimacies add spice that heightens their excitement. With the danger of discovery never far away, versatility and adaptability to uncomfortable or compromising situations is vital. Members of the Mile High Club for airborne sexual adventurers and lovers who manage to operate on the back seat of an MGB at 70 mph automatically belong to the Naughty-Sporty group. They often advertise by placing jokey stickers in their car windows saying 'Wind-Surfers Do It Standing Up' or variations on that theme.

The Naughty-Sports are out for fun and aim to please their partners, but romance with them is of necessity often rushed and not for the faint-hearted.

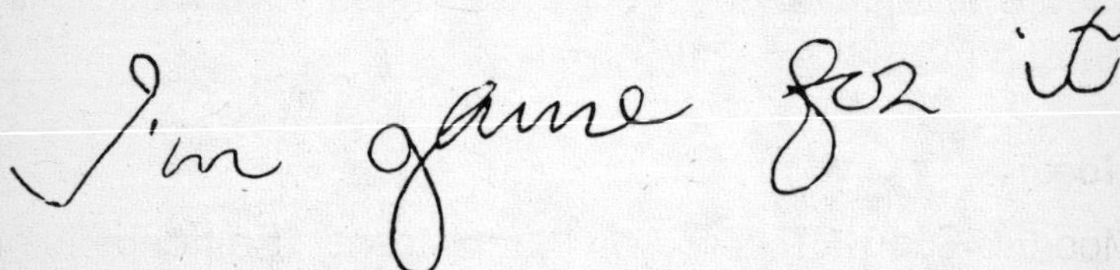

Naughty Sporties write quickly and with a mixed slant. Letters are broad and m's and n's have pointed tops. The 't' bar crossings rise. The baseline bobs up and down and the lower zone is dominant in their writing.

Bionic Bedmates

These Action Men and Wonder-Women have amazing

stamina and staying power. Always full of zest and zeal, their high performance physical urges are strong and urgent and their action replays are just as powerful and important as their first clinch. When really necessary – if discovered in flagrante delicto by jealous wives or husbands – they can leap to safety with one bound, shin down the drainpipe and hurl themselves out of harm's way without working up so much as a bead of sweat on their brow. Sexual satisfaction with a Bionic Bedmate is guaranteed, so long as you can stand the pace – which is always switched on to fast forward, with the promise of more repeats than even a whole week of BBC television.

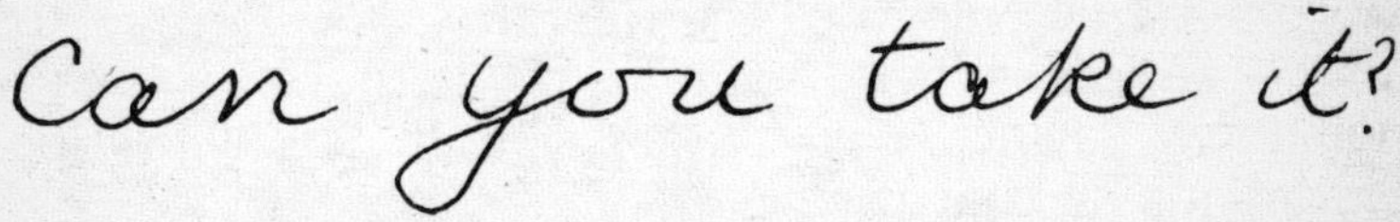

Bionic Bedmates write with distinct pressure and slant to the right. Their letters are connected and while middle and upper zones are balanced, lower zones will show a pronounced lengthening.

Moodies

Moodies can be mean – or magnificent. It all depends on their whim of the moment, which can change at the drop of a hint or an unguarded remark.

Their partners rarely know what to expect, from a wild exuberant and exciting bedmate to a touchy, irritable lover whose performance is lacklustre or lacking and whose sulks cannot be appeased, won round or teased even for the sake of pleasure.

Unhappy children from unhappy pasts, they have become unpredictable adults governed by their erratic and shredded emotions. They love in order to be hateful,

Moodies' partners rarely know what to expect...

as that is their way of constantly testing the strength of anyone else's love and loyalty.

Thriving on uncertainty, they swing in behaviour from Dracula to Angel. Relationships with Moodies are always on/off unpredictable affairs and last just as long as their partners' nerves can withstand the strain.

---

not tonight Josephine

Broken romances reinforce the Moodies in their bitter expectations ensuring that subsequent relationships are primed to follow the same disastrous and destructive course even from the start.

Moody writers display a mix of upright and right slants. The lines rise and fall, the pressure varies and some letters are disconnected. The length of lower zones fluctuates.

Potency Problem Playmate – Men Only

If the sex drive dwindles, leading to a lack of interest, failure, lapses or collapses, the male often turns his back on his regular partner. Unable to face the fact that his potency power is weak, especially if he used to enjoy the reputation of a sexual stud, he will often mentally offload the blame on his bedmate.

Feeling threatened and diminished, he can opt for increasingly bizarre and outrageous sex in an effort to boost his flagging excitement and restore his drive. Group sex, stage displays, erotic movies, gadgets and aids may be used as props to bolster interest.

Handwriting reflects changes in physical responses, acting as an early-warning system so help can be sought before the problem becomes deep-seated and difficult to treat, or before deteriorating relations with regular partners threaten to cause rifts.

Potency Problem Playmates write with light pen pressure, particularly in the lower zone. Lower loops can

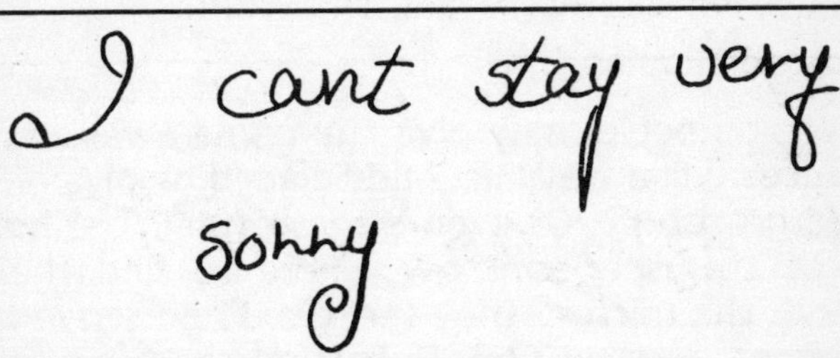

If the sex drive dwindles... the male often turns his back on his regular partner.

be either open and enrolled, twisted or very long and lean with the upstroke parallel and close to the downstroke. Their 't' bar crosses are weak.

Middle-Aged Hippies

Their pension books may give the game away, but their appearances will always lie. Middle-aged hippies refuse to grow old gracefully. Or even disgracefully. The male and female of this species know where to find their best friend – in the mirror. They feel good and strive hard to look as good as they feel. Both find sanctuary under a

Middle-Aged Hippies refuse to grow old gracefully. Or even disgracefully

sunlamp to maintain a St Tropez tan all year long even in Tottenham. He keeps his hand-stitched toupée in place (even during moments of passion). She makes coquettish passes at her gay hairdresser even as he colours her grey hair. Contact lenses are tinted and teeth of immaculate porcelain are firmly rivetted to cover rotting stumps. The Middle-Aged Hippy's second-best friend is their surgeon, who can lift and tuck everything that sags or bags into place, from pouches under the eyes to hernias carefully arranged into surgical corsets or varicose veins wrapped like Egyptian mummies in support stockings.

These are the lovers who insist on dimmed lights and who take furtive peeps in the hand mirror (always within reach) to ensure passion has not dislodged so much as a false eyelash. Their image is and always will be their prime concern, and despite their pacemakers, they grimly aim to remain eternally young at heart.

Middle-Aged Hippies' writing is left slanting with higher upper zones. The lower zone is short and repressed yet the middle zone is very full. The writing looks pasty and childish with letter size growing at the end of words.

Sozzled Lovers – or Who Put the Randy in Brandy?

A hangover is this lover's answer to hang-ups. They usually need a drink – or two or three or thirteen – to turn themselves on as there is nothing like alcohol to loosen their inhibitions.

Yet drunks lose the critical judgement they need to decide when they have gone over the nicely relaxed and loosened-up point.

Their boozy, whoozy brain tells them they have the confidence and sexual *oomph* to turn in a virtuoso performance.

Their bodies simply refuse to cooperate, as any victim of Brewer's Droop will testify.

The reality of a habitual sozzled lover's sex life is not round after round of wild drunken orgies but night after night sleeping it off alone leaving their partners bitter and unsatisfied.

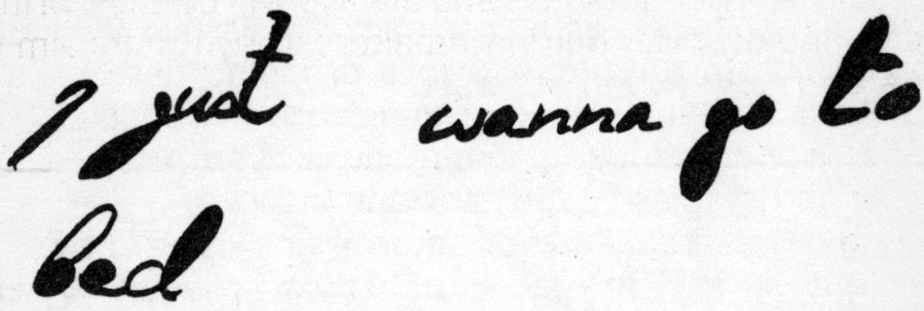

Sozzled lovers' writing has a marked right slant and looks pasty, smeary and blotchy. Upper zones are long and inflated and lower zones are long. Ovals and loops are filled with ink and the lines are irregular.

Drunks lose the critical judgement they need to decide when they have gone over the nicely relaxed and loosened up point.

Flirts

The compulsive flirt knows how to tease and tempt and can't resist any opportunity to try the turn-on game. He fancies his chances, as a debonair, irresistible lady-killer who can charm any woman into dropping her guard or underwear for him – even grannies are fair sport.

She is a glorious glamour puss who uses winks, wiggles and giggles to enchant and enslave.

Suggestive and saucy or smooth and subtle, the flirt plays out a stylish game of trivial pursuit. Risqué conversations conducted in secret whispers are potent aphrodisiacs. Long, smouldering looks stoke up the emotional fires to flashpoint.

They are full of passionate promise but when tested, the charm and chat are just a charade. *He* often turns out to be all mouth and no trousers. *She* gets her kicks from mental foreplay, not nitty-gritty grappling.

For lovers of flirts, it adds up to an armful of hot air and disappointment.

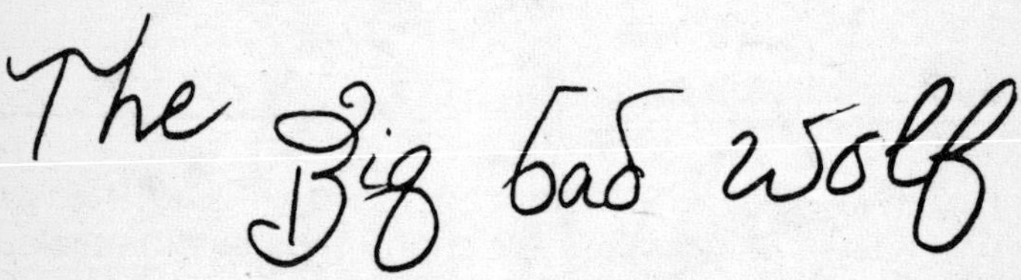

Flirts add flags to the tops of their 'd's and 't's. Loops and scrolls abound. The writing has a rightward slant, lines are wavy and there is a mix of loops and single downstrokes in upper and lower zones.

The Unfaithful

To lovers with roving eyes, monogamy is a bored game for

two. Infidelity is simply irresistible. Unfaithful lovers are readily available and always on the market, believing stolen pleasures are always sweeter. They just have to play around, but they may not be as clever at covering their tracks as they think. The inky clues to the many varieties of the unfaithful are easy to spot. Within the all-embracing arm of the unfaithful come the following distinct categories.

1. *Secretive Randy Rovers* take care to ensure that their regular partners stay blissfully ignorant of their bedhopping games. They are evasive about their sexual movements to avoid being caught out but in the delicious secrecy of snatched forbidden passion they let themselves go freely.

Secretive Randy Rovers

2. Unfaithful Lovers who play *Lord or Lady Bountiful* want to give happiness to many by sharing and baring their all.

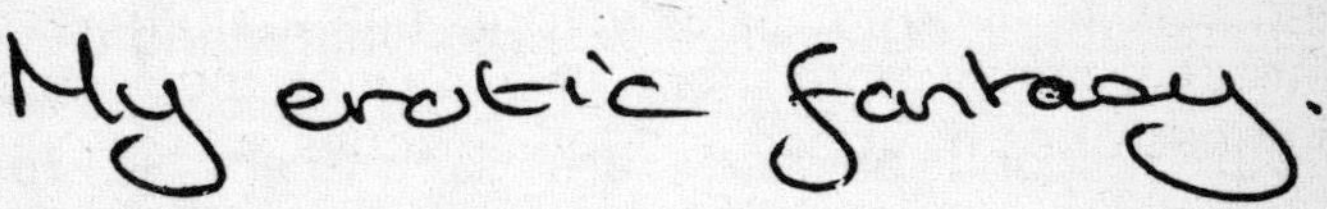

Lord or Lady Bountiful

3. *Restless Rovers* love change. They are always ready to

change partners so their sex life is a dizzy, adventurous whirl. When the music stops, they must have someone new to captivate, conquer then kiss goodbye.

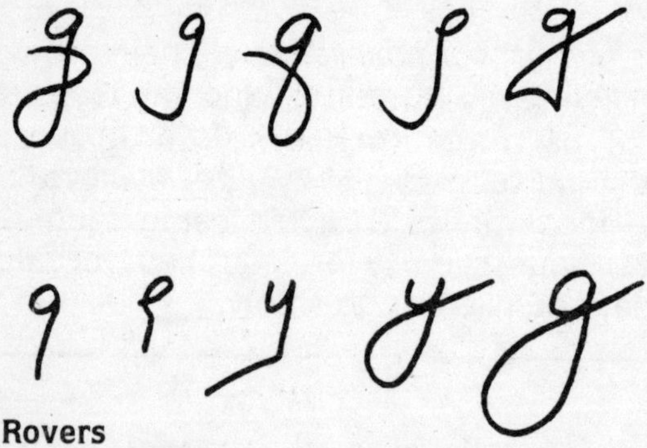

Restless Rovers

4. *Experimental Rovers* not only love sex with someone new – they also prefer unusual positions.

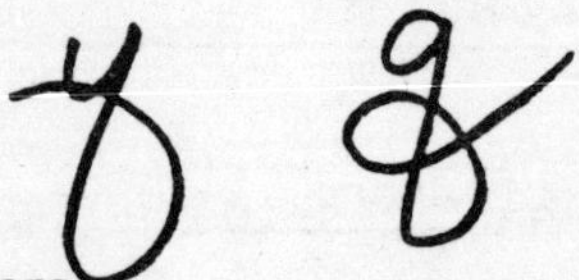

Experimental Rovers

5. *Helpless Rovers* tumble into infidelity because they are vulnerable to the wiles, winks, whims and desires of others. If someone gives them the eye, they can't help but respond as they are so susceptible to sexy temptation and stimulation. It is impossible for them to say no.

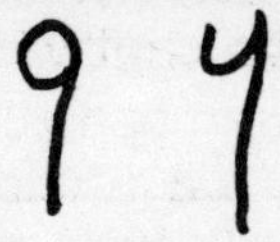

Helpless Rovers

6. *Expert Unfaithful Lovers* show their prowess if their lines of handwriting mingle and the loops are full and rounded. They are certainly unfaithful – but oh so good at it, and never kiss and tell as a point of honour.

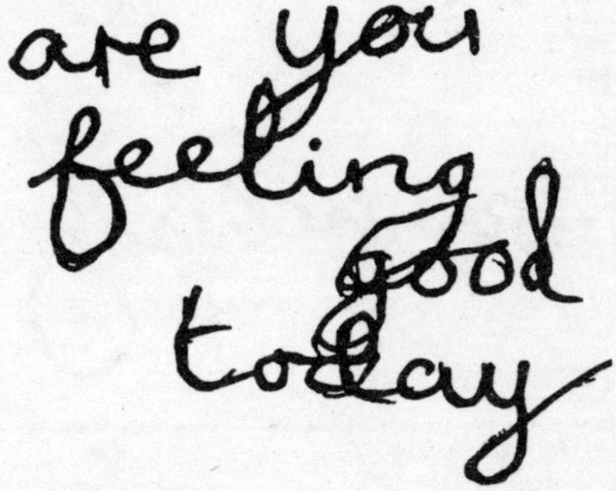

Expert Unfaithful Lovers

Forbidden Fruit Pluckers

The message they can't resist is one that reads: *Trespassers Will Be Prosecuted.* Forbidden Fruit Pluckers always want what is not rightfully theirs, and if danger studs the route to forbidden fruit, the more eager they are to reach it, no matter whose property they encroach.

Looking and admiring from afar is not their style. They have to touch, feel and make their mark, rather like a dog marking territory.

If the pursuit is too easy, the game becomes boring, as they thrive on challenge and overcoming odds. The harder the goal and the higher the danger stakes, the more attractive and urgent the need to conquer.

Anyone who conducts a torrid affair with a married neighbour, stalks the boss's wife or his virgin daughter, or sets out to unfrock the vicar is a vicarious Forbidden Fruit Plucker.

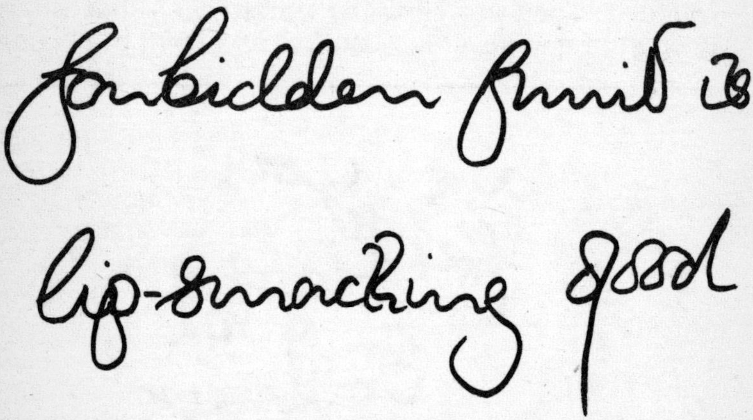

Forbidden Fruit Pluckers have upright writing and leave wide left margins. Letters are broad and lines are wavy. The writing looks pasty. A variety of loops and formations will be seen in the lower zone. Rising lines are over-accentuated and writing size is large.

Unstoppable and Insatiable Pistol-Packing Partners

Hot-blooded and impetuous, it takes just a suggestive remark, a lustful thought, or the merest glimpse of a sexy leg, an untethered bosom, a manly chest or a bulging crotch to whip up strong and uncontrollable desires.

Always poised under starter's orders, these easily

aroused lovers respond to a sexual suggestion like a bullet out of a gun.

Driven and dominated by the physical, both male and female of the species seek urgent gratification with little or no consideration of delicacy, style, timing or convenience, let alone self-control. They are such fast workers, it is impossible for them to hold themselves back. Sex is the trigger that fires them and their target – rapid satisfaction – is reached in no time at all.

Ever alert for sexual input, they can't resist touching body shapes or suggestive material with their hands. They are always in a rush and cannot delay their responses.

Pistol-Packing Partners rarely have time to jump out of their clothes to enjoy more leisurely naked romps, preferring to take their pleasure whenever they find it. Like an automatic rifle, they are instantly recharged and reloaded ready for repeat action replays. It doesn't seem to affect the quality of enjoyment of sex for them, as power and peak performance at high speed is the essence of their response.

They frequently feature as the fabled lustful stallions whose superhuman revelations launch a million pulp paperbacks, or the soft-porn heroines who can seemingly satisfy a battalion of sex-starved soldiers in one session.

Though rare, they do exist in reality. Mother Nature's hand simply slipped when handling out their supply of highly charged sexual batteries.

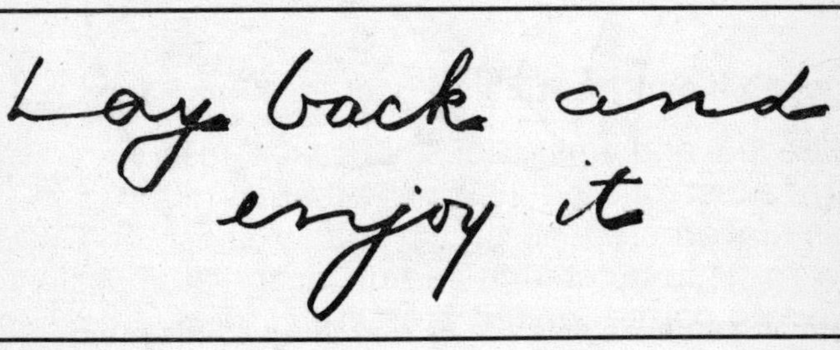

The Unstoppable and Insatiable show a marked right slant and use heavy pressure. Letters are broad and connected though they look angular. End strokes are thickened.

Mummy's Boy

The sexual urges of Mummy's Boy got knotted and throttled by his mother's apron strings at an early age.

Even Oedipus was a traitor to his mater by comparison.

Mother is the first person he thinks of when he wakes in the morning. Her whims and orders are obeyed without question. Her comfort and happiness are his anxious concern. He feels it is the least he can do for her in return for the smother love showered upon him as a baby.

Mother pandered to his every whim, filling his playpen with goodies at the merest whimper, slavishly giving her undivided and unstinting attention to him, without

No woman can ever displace or match up to his mum.

allowing any involvement or interference from anyone else, especially Father. She shooed away the bully boys and the bogeymen and ladled chicken soup and barley down him to keep even nasty germs at bay.

In adulthood, no woman can ever displace or match up to his mum. Unfamiliar females are a frightening race who mock and boss, snigger and betray him. At least, that's what mummy says when he confides in her his feelings about the girls he has met. No girl will ever be good enough for her boy, and no woman in her right mind should contemplate taking on the challenge of being the Other Woman in his life.

Mummy always knows best, because Mum's the word.

You can recognize a Mummy's Boy by his soft, pudgy and well moisturized skin, immaculately clean nails and fastidious habits.

Mummy's Boy's handwriting shows a marked left slant. The style is copybook with spirals in capitals or hooks. The middle zone is large and lower zone formations look like cradles.

Sugar Daddy's Girl

Sweet, soft and sugary, even candy floss wouldn't melt in her mouth. Her expression is wide-eyed, innocent and angelic. Her nose is a delicate button and her lips cherry-ripe and cherubic.

As a toddler, she lisped her way to daddy's heart and twisted him round her pretty podgy finger.

As an adult, she latches on to an older man to carry on the role of spoiling her and keeping her cocooned and cossetted in comfort away from the harsh economic pressures of the world outside.

She can't bear to be deprived of any of life's little luxuries, from glittering trinkets and furs to the essential Ferrari. Only a rich ageing lothario can afford to pick up the bill. He needs her as mascot and testimony to his riches, youthfulness and virility. The price she has to pay for all the gorgeous goodies only money can buy is to ooze reassurance with every simpering smile.

His wrinkles don't matter, so long as his wallet continues to bulge.

Underneath her cute exterior beats a heart of pure granite. She knows that an old fool and his money are soon parted.

Sugar Daddy's Girl shows large money bags in the lower zone. Middle zone is large and the writing is pasty and upright with a tendency to lean to the right. She leaves narrow left margins, enrols letters and displays a variety of hooks, claws and cats' paws. End strokes are sharp.

Premature Lovers

Easily excited but too quick to sustain a satisfying sex session, the performance of a Premature Lover is always a literal let-down.

They long to hold back, but their instant climaxes, unplanned and unexpected, always break the speed limit.

Their problem is nearly always founded in their early sexual experiences. Guilty grappling behind the bike shed, furtive fumblings in the cinema back seat and high-tension petting on the sofa when the family were out – all help to create a pattern of response that associates sex with speed to avoid the terror of possible discovery. The wham-bam-thank-you-mam approach of snatched sex seems safest and preferable to the lasting shame of being caught with their pants down.

But then, in the deep, deep peace of the double bed after the hurly-burly of the chaise longue, they find the hasty habit lingers.

Inwardly, they are unhappy, concerned and self-conscious at their lack of control. It makes them feel selfish and guilty of being unable to hold back long enough to satisfy their partner. Outwardly, they may try bluff, bluster and bravado to mask their problems.

Common cover-up tricks include childishly blaming their partners for their own sexual shortcomings.

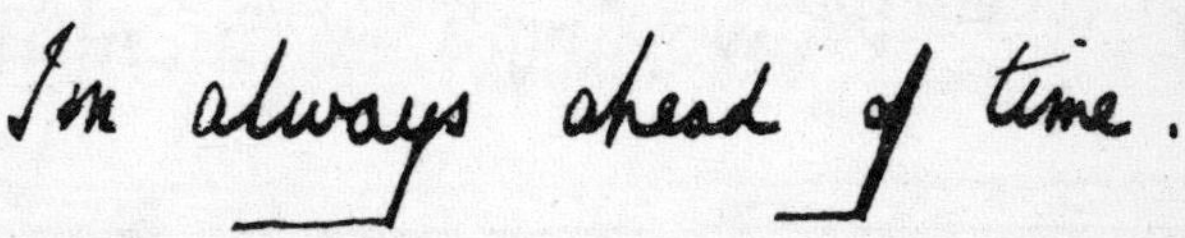

Premature Lovers' writing is sharp, lean and narrow. There is a marked right slant with drooping or falling lines. In the lower zone, there is a leftward and horizontal movement. Covering strokes are added to letters.

Fusspots and Fault-Finders

Niggling, nagging and nit-picking come easily to Fusspot Fault-Finders. Ever watchful of the imperfection of others, every slip or sin is noted and taken down to be used in evidence against their partner.

They criticize the personal habits and manners, as well as the appearance and performance of their lovers. Being a critical nit-picker is actually a full-time occupation and they can't resist finding flaws and faults both in bed and out.

On the domestic front this makes them petty tyrants. On an intimate level, their incessant search for imperfection in others is a great psychological cover. Picking partners to pieces is reassuring to the Fusspot Fault-Finder as the more they downgrade others, the higher they boost their self-image.

They can drive their lovers potty – and that is just where their problems originate. Mothers who were over-zealous and over-anxious with toilet-training; who scolded and fussed when their squeaky clean baby chewed worms in the garden or mixed mudpies in the playpen produce Fusspots.

Fusspots' writing is spidery and features extra long starting strokes. The 't' bars point downwards. Writing size can be either small, or large with a small medium zone. Triangles are formed in the lower zone. The writing is upright with left tendencies and letters are disconnected.

Biters, Scratchers and Sexual Slave-Drivers

Sinking their dentures into a lover's exposed flesh or

scoring their skin with lethal claws at critical moments in a sexual clinch smacks of raw, rampant, primitive and predatory animal power.

The marks form a message tattooed for all the world to see. It reads: This One is Mine.

What Biters, Scratchers and Sexual Slave-Drivers all have in common is a shrewd instinctive understanding of beastly bully-boy tactics to force their beloved to knuckle under. Passion is their cover for forcing a weaker and vulnerable partner to submit.

They have honed down hurt to a fine art. Scratchers grow their nails to claw-like talons to ensure maximum effect. Biters don't take trouble to take their teeth out at night before snuggling up for a nibble.

They are actually hard taskmasters who expect and demand perfection from their mates. Fierce rages can erupt if they meet any obstacle or upset that thwarts them.

Clues to their proclivities can be found in the unusual objects they collect, such as swords, instruments of torture, old-fashioned cutting implements and penknives.

Their handwriting gives the ghoullish game away.

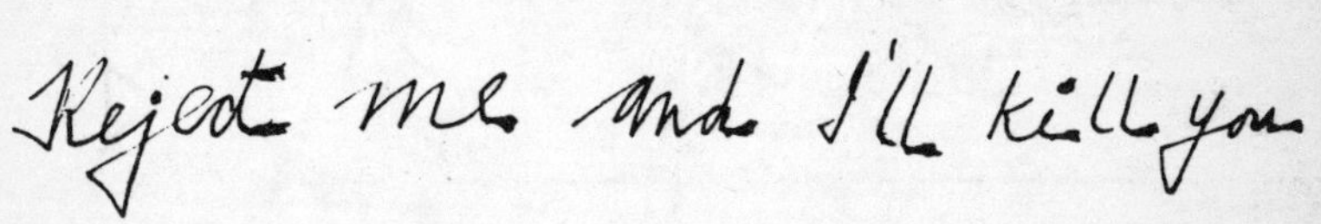

Sharp or calligraphic writing is the mark of the Biters, Scratchers and Sexual Slave-Drivers. They make angular connections. Their 't' bars thicken at the end of the stroke and point downwards. Lines mingle, 'i' dots are low and capitals have flourishes.

The Femme Fatale

The key to the Femme Fatale is her need to be the object

of desire and the secret fantasy of all.

You can smell her approaching from a hundred yards. She oozes perfume from every pore as if she had applied it with a garden hose. Once the nose has picked up her scent, the senses take up the trail. She always looks glamorous and is never caught out in a grubby housecoat and curlers, no matter how dire the emergency.

She would always choose to go out of the house wearing no knickers rather than no make-up. Make-up applied in careful layers is the war-paint she wears in the battle of the sexes. And she never loses.

Every trick in the trade is used to project her earthy image. Clothes in soft sensuous fabrics that men want to touch and caress are chosen with care to cling and enhance, flatter and tease.

Every trick in the trade is used to project her earthy image.

See-through is her trump card. Heaving cleavage is the ace tucked up her sleeveless all-revealing camisole. High heels ensure her walk is always slinky and willowy enough to create a wiggle.

The Femme Fatale rivets attention and revels in it, heading for nudist camps, fashionable health hydros and topless beaches to make her spectacular appearances.

Her handwriting style simply amplifies the message of eroticism she shrieks through her body language. And she never ever signs so much as a cheque in a common, chewed-up ballpoint, but always uses a stylish expensive pen.

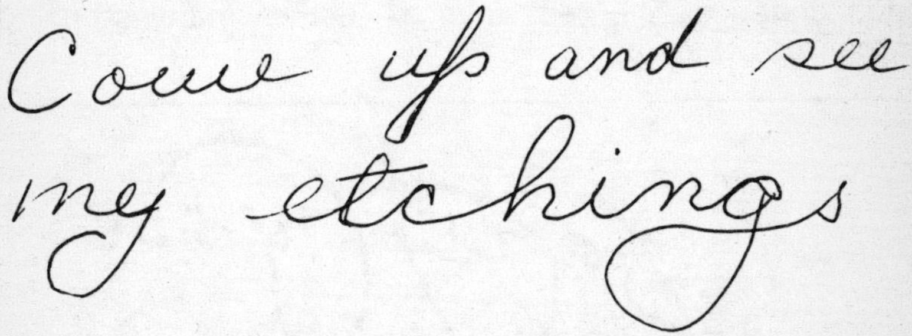

The Femme Fatale uses lots of loops and garlands on her large, full and rounded writing. The middle zone is large, and lower zone loops are very full but can be incomplete.

The Nymphomaniac

She is the lady who has launched a thousand quips at stag nights, rugby club celebrations or wherever lusty men gather to swop notes and boasts.

Her sexual quest is satisfaction, though she can never find it. That doesn't, however, stop this game girl from trying.

Restlessly she seeks outside relief from the anxiety and high tension she feels inside. Medics recognize that the problem and its resolution lie in her head, not her erogenous zones. Yet the nymphomaniac's fabled reputation marches on as the fantasy of every man's erotic dream: The girl who just can't say No.

Discrimination is not one of her virtues. She revels in pick-up situations with strangers, from lay-bys with lorry drivers to alley encounters with all-comers. The world is actually full of welcome opportunities for sexual adventures with any Tom, Dick or Willie.

Powered by her compulsion and frustration, she looks for change and change again.

Sexual Shangri-la always shimmers and beckons in the dim distance. She sees men as just so many stepping stones on the way.

I fancy you again, and again and again

The Nymphomaniac has very distorted and exaggerated lower zones with bizarre formations. Loops are inflated in lower and upper zones. The writing has an artificial fullness and features mixed slants. The 'i' dots are missing and phallic symbols are woven into the writing.

Excuse Experts

Headaches were invented for the Excuse Experts. With a lower sex drive than the norm, Excuse Experts don't feel the need to exercise their carnal equipment more often than they feel necessary, and that is usually confined to birthdays, high days and holidays.

Excuse Experts don't feel the need to exercise their carnal equipment more often than they feel necessary.

One of their favourite phrases is: 'Hanky-panky is all very well, but there is a time and a place for everything.' The second favourite is to deny that a little bit of what you fancy does you good.

They are convinced their sexual performance is as much as any decent person could need, and if pressed by frustrated partners, the excuses just come rolling out in a litany.

'I'm too tired', 'My back aches', 'Not now, the children are still awake', 'I've an important meeting in the morning and need my sleep', 'You'll crumple my new suit/frock', and the crowning cliché: 'I've got a headache'.

Their sexual safety curtain comes down immediately after the excuses are accepted.

There are nothing like delaying tactics to keep a problem at bay, and the more they are pushed the more elaborate their excuses become. If forced into a corner, their fallback position is an attack in the form of a reproach or accusation: 'How could you be so beastly/selfish/uncaring ...?'.

By then the simple matter of sexual expression is utterly irrelevant in the ensuing blazing row, on any topic, that follows.

---

my teeth are

hurting

Excuse Experts write with a right slant but lower zone strokes lean to the left. Their 't' bars are placed behind the stem and the 'i' dot behind the 'i'. There is an avoidance of loops, and letters are partially disconnected with sudden narrowness.

Shockers

Always the first to suggest swinging naked from the chandelier, dressing up in edible or incredible undies, or stripping naked and streaking with no knickers at Twickers, the Shockers are game for any dare.

Outrageous thrills are an erotic essential to their sexual exploits.

Shockers need to stand out in a crowd and will go to any lengths to keep all eyes focused on them. Any stunt will be pulled to create and capture an audience.

They get high when others gasp with horror; they revel when shyer souls cringe and turn pink with embarrassment. Notoriety is the flame that fans their wild urge to act out their sexual fantasies in public.

Shockers need to stand out in a crowd.

The more unpredictable the outcome, the more exciting and enticing the act.

At heart, a Shocker is a very special showman whose satisfaction comes from knowing their partner has experienced a night they will always remember.

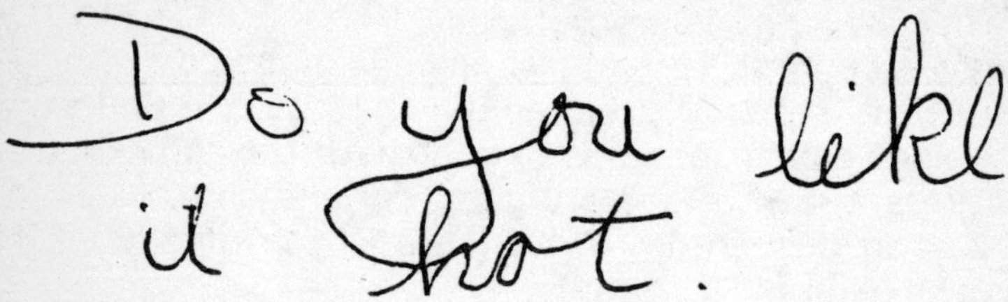

Shockers' writing is irregular and large with a left slant. The letters grow in size. Looping is usual and the baseline uneven.

Loyal Lovers

Loyal lovers look forward to holding hands with their partner at the Darby & Joan club, decades after plighting their troth. And they still only have eyes for their beloved.

No one and nothing rocks their romantic boat as they aim to stay faithful through thick and thin.

They have no secrets from their mate because they have no guilty activities they need to hide. They trust their partner completely and believe in them and support them utterly. With this unity of purpose, response and ambition comes a sexual compatibility. Each Loyal Lover knows how to keep their partner happy and pleasure comes from entwining each other in a tight, exclusive knot of satisfying love.

With such deep, meaningful and harmonious feeling

comes respect and understanding.

Loyal lovers are basically balanced and integrated. Single-minded and with no hang-ups, they never air their marital dirty linen in public places.

Temptation outside the marriage doesn't rate a second glance. They are simply not in the market as infidelity is unthinkable.

They are truly yours faithfully.

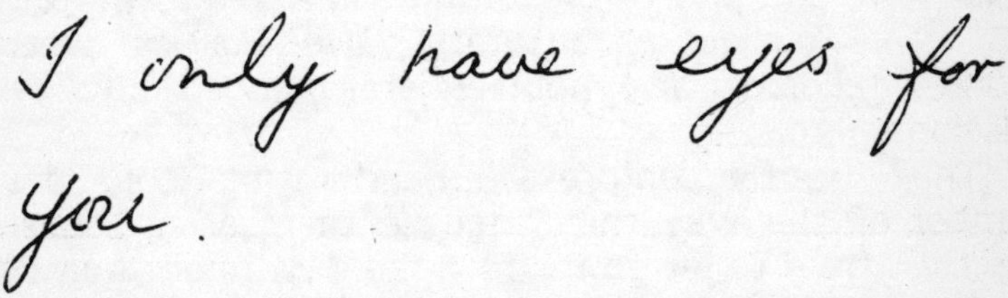

Loyal Lovers show a right slant with full lower zones and completed loops in the upper and lower zones. The lines are clearly spaced with no mingling. A few starting strokes can be seen here and there as well as extended end strokes. The writing is fairly well connected and can be pasty or distinct.

The Inhibited and Repressed

The inhibited and repressed store their emotions in screw-top jars with tightly sealed lids.

These potentially explosive devices are stored in their unconscious minds, a habit instilled into them from childhood when they were taught to keep their sexual feelings firmly under control as sensuousness and 'dirty' play were sinful.

These successfully suppressed natural feelings ferment away causing nervous tension and low ego energy. Desires are still on the boil, but with instinct thwarted the temperature rises in the internal pressure cooker.

No wonder the Inhibited and Repressed dare not let go.

As a precaution, they undress in the dark. Sexual activity is undertaken, if at all, perfunctorily with lights turned off. Personal thoughts are kept private. Sex is a sensitive taboo subject in conversation.

As a second defence measure, they channel misplaced sexual energies and the resulting frightening frustration into other outlets as a safety valve. Politics, worthy causes, religions and hobbies are plunged into with missionary zeal.

Their tightly compressed handwriting loops are a symbol of the way they squeeze themselves together tightly, afraid to let go for fear the dam might burst.

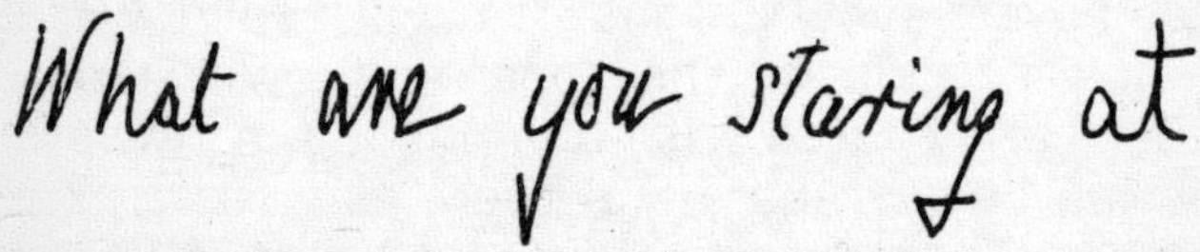

The Inhibited have upright or left slant and their writing shows narrowness, and leanness, some angularity and cramped letters. Lower zones are pointed. The style is very regular and rigid with no rhythm.

The Sexually Selfish and Stingy

The sexually Selfish and Stingy don't believe in giving themselves willy-nilly as the mood takes them.

Love is rationed and stored for special occasions, not gorged with lusty gusto like a free hot dinner.

They give their affections in sparingly small portions

as if the supply were shortly to run out.

Close physical contact is worked out in advance to suit themselves, and spontaneity is discouraged.

Love is rationed and stored for special occasions...

They rationalize the rationing by arguing that over-indulgence is rash and wasteful, that anticipation sharpens the appetite and that anything worth having is worth waiting for – until they are ready to give it, that is.

Playing hard to get and denying their partner the goodies on demand actually gives them a kick, even if their sleeping partner is sex-starved in the process, 'Not tonight, Josephine' will be their response unless and until they are feeling ready and randy. Sexual service has to be earned.

Great strength of will is used to deny their partners the pleasure they seek. The Sexually Selfish and Stingy will not be coaxed or cajoled, caressed or cursed into changing their minds.

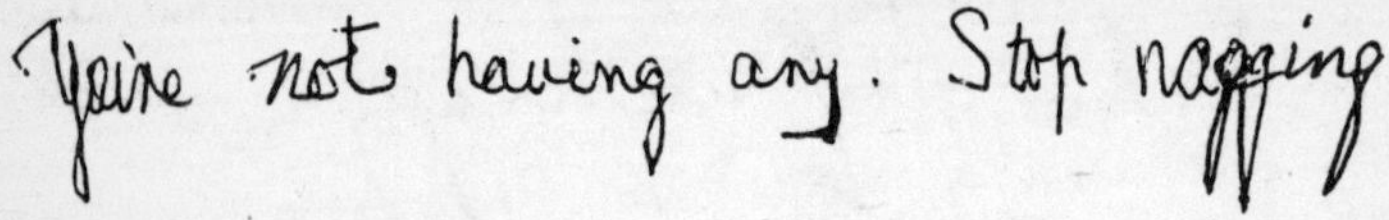

The Sexually Selfish and Stingy write with a left slant and add hooks to starting strokes. Middle zone is large, end strokes curl leftwards and they leave narrow spaces between words and lines.

The Unfulfilled

The Unfulfilled long to find the key that fits the lock that opens up the door to ultimate satisfaction and gratification. But they feel that nature has filled them with an invisible chastity belt that denies them ultimate pleasure.

The Unfulfilled become fretful and irritable knowing that they are missing out. Their requirements are basic and their urges eager, yet they can't help feeling they are failing to achieve the sensational.

In the right atmosphere, with someone they fancy, they can summon the necessary excitement. But then the climax is such a let-down they feel incomplete.

Life can become one round of different one-night stands to find the magic key to solve the problem. Unless they do find a regular relationship, they can rust up and lose their touch altogether, becoming brittle and bitter in the process.

The resulting hang-up spills into everyday life making them feel discontented, cynical, distrusting and disappointed. They rarely seem to find much joy in daily living.

The Unfulfilled's writing is lean and narrow. The upper zone is tall, the middle zone small and some lower loops are uncompleted with some crossing very low on the long

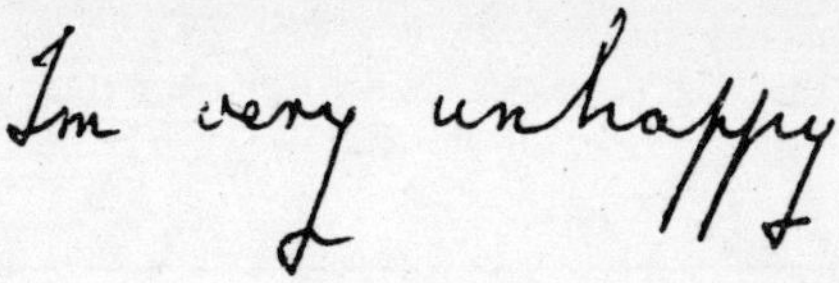

downstroke with the addition of a droopy 'tail'. The style is angular and the writing size small. Heavy pressure is used and baselines fall.

Slobs and Sluts

Members of the slob and slut set revel in glorious, grubby grime. They ooze sweat from every pore, which keeps their hands clammy enough to leave greasy paw prints on everyone they encounter. And they can't resist having a feel, with bottom-pinching and groping in the dark their favourite turn-ons.

Slovenliness is soothing and comfortable. Birthday suits need only minimum care and raw body odours are regarded as the perfect natural pheromone to attract a mate. Deodorants, perfume and mouthwashes are an irrelevance to them as they cannot detect any unpleasantness in their own scent signals.

Slobs and sluts only manage to look spruced up and clean momentarily before their natural state reasserts itself. Their spectacles are always steamy. They are more at ease slopping around in old familiar and tatty clothes than stiff spanking new ones, and can manage to make even pristine outfits look instantly shabby with grimy tidemarks at collar and cuffs, lipstick smudges, cigarette ash spills, stains or sweaty, scurvy, scruffy patches.

Dirty thoughts match their dirty appearance. Sex-play is always referred to as 'mucking about'. Smutty postcards and porn movies exert a great attraction and dirty tricks from novelty shops appeal to their base sense of humour.

Birthday suits need only minimum care and rare body odours are regarded as the perfect natural pheromone...

Their bedtime habits are just as slovenly. Sheets are rarely changed and between them you will find slummy refuse from crumbs to old cornplasters.

Slobs and sluts are best happily matched with each other so they can luxuriate in their own low standards of hygiene without inciting or inviting criticism or disgust.

Slobs and Sluts form smeary, smudgy, blotchy and pasty strokes. The writing is irregular, ovals and small loops are filled with ink and the style looks untidy. Mixed

slant, varying pressure and untidy capital letter forms are used.

Disillusioned Dreamers

When stark reality becomes too much to bear, Disillusioned Dreamers flee to a make-believe world of their dreams. In their castles in the air, open twenty-four hours a day, partners are perfectly gorgeous, passion is boundless, sex is spaced-out and sensational and life simply heavenly.

Back on earth with a bump, sexual situations knock them flat. Disillusioned Dreamers fail to find fulfilment. Half the time they don't know what they are looking for anyway. Disappointed and disconsolate, they never make the most of what they have got.

Their partners don't stand a chance. How could mere mortals match up to expectations when ideals and aims forged in fantasy and dreams are so impossibly high?

At the end of the day, escapism becomes a welcome relief from the sordid, sorry state of affairs in the real world of relationships. In their mind, Disillusioned Dreamers can rise above it all as Superstud and Wonderwoman. In reality, between the sheets, they are so heavenly minded they are of little earthly use.

Disillusioned Dreamers' writing shows exaggerated fullness with massive florid upper zone loops. Middle zone

letters are small and lean and the lower zone is full. Writing slants to the left and the baseline shows an erratic and convex curve.

Disillusioned Dreamers flee to a make-believe world...

The Frigid

Hugging Ms Frigid is like cuddling up to a pack of deep-frozen fish fingers: the response is just as icy. She gives sex the cold shoulder and any man who tries to thaw out her feelings gets frozen out.

Since her first sexual experience was unsatisfactory and frightening, she won't chance a second. Subsequent sexual suggestion is shrugged aside. She is not readily aroused and will not allow any man near enough to try to kindle the flame. Interlopers who dare warm her up risk being sent to the emotional equivalent of Siberia for their trouble.

She is truly untouchable, with cold contempt stored within her to wither anyone who tries.

Eroticism and sexual energy are converted into safer pastimes and hobbies that do not require rampant hot-blooded responses.

She may climb to the top of her profession or take comfort from crusades, good causes or running a

Ms Frigid gives sex the cold shoulder.

sanctuary for homeless cats to compensate for her deep-frozen and forgotten sexuality.

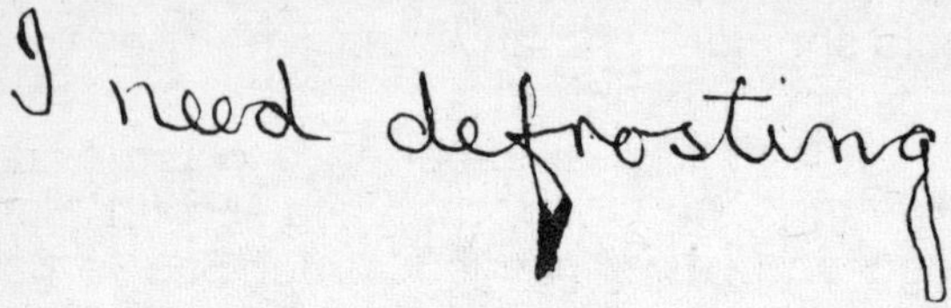

The Frigid write with a lack of rhythm. Letters are extremely sharp and thin and the strokes rigid. Lower zone loops are weak and of strange formations, usually with loops uncompleted.

The Frustrated

She is chained to the kitchen sink, part of the fixtures and fittings of the home. Taken for granted, unappreciated, bored and dull, her daily life is a drudge.

Every day brings the same old routine from washing on Monday to shopping on Friday and sex on Saturday.

Not that she complains. The pattern of her life is clear and uncomplicated and she knows what is coming and when, so why expect sexual fireworks in a humdrum relationship that lost its fizzle for her long ago?

But she yearns for it all the same, and she knows how to get her kicks without causing a ripple on the happy home scene ... The milkman has plenty of bottle and the postman has her stamp of approval. The plumber knows how to turn her tap on and the electrician's shock tactics make the sparks fly.

He is factory or office fodder, a reliable, dutiful, responsible time-server who is useful at work but no go-getter. Life both at home and at work is routine and predictable. He thinks about, but shrinks from opportunities to kick over the traces and quit his dull job or shake up his plodding marriage. He is actually ground too far into the rut to dare to bother to change.

But inside him the spark of defiance and frustration still flares, even though he has to pay to satisfy it with anonymous encounters at massage or prostitute's parlours.

Vicarious secret sex with no strings blows away the cobwebs from dull and dreary lives for the frustrated and unfulfilled.

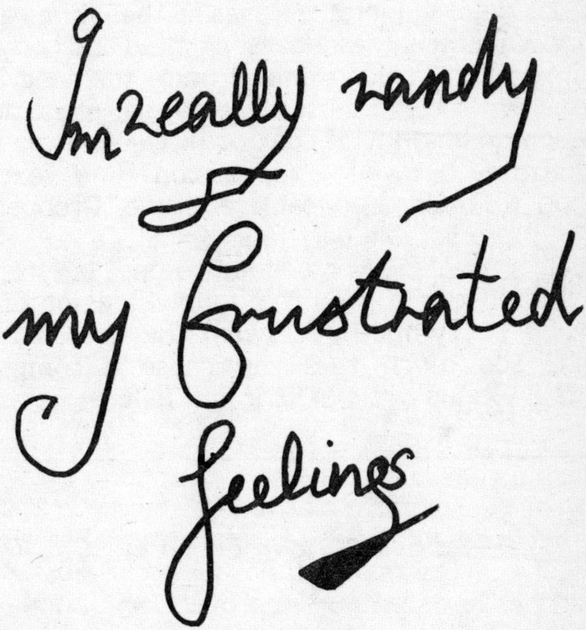

The Frustrated form large lower zones and small middle zones. Lower zone loops are incomplete, swing to the left and vary in length. They also have ticks on the ends. Letters show sporadic narrowness. Covering strokes are used.

The Droops

These temperamental trapeze artists find sex a tightrope experience. When feeling on top of the world, they fly high. When feeling down, their sexual performance slithers to a depressed droop.

While the going is good, they are exceptionally rampant and virile, making up for lost time and pride. The drive to prove themselves gives them added power and passion as they strive to master their partner – and their problem.

But they are vulnerable slaves to the whims and wilts of their own internal responses. As mind and body have to move in perfectly synchronized unity for good sex, any emotional wobble can cause a spectacular physical drop or flop which no amount of coaxing or cajoling can cure.

Swinging between repression and expression according to their changeable attitude, Droopers make sexually unpredictable partners.

If you are wedded or bedded to one, be prepared to make the most of a good thing when it is on offer, and shrug and be sympathetic when the notorious droops descend. Too much fuss can cause a complex that prompts a vicious circle of fear and failure.

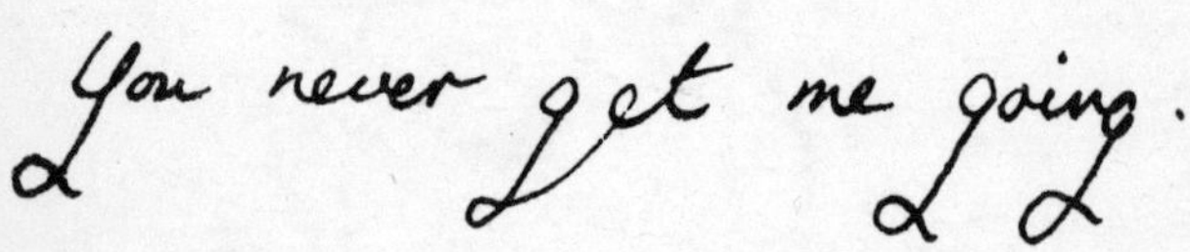

The Droops write with weak pressure and both capitals and letters are narrow and sharp. Covering strokes are used. Lower zones are ticked and/or look wilted at the ends.

Fakers

With their motto 'If you don't feel it, fake it', these actors and actresses of Oscar-winning standard put on a polished performance.

Their aim is to convince their partner that they are hot stuff; veritable towering infernos of passion.

With the aid of expressive sound-effects, ranging from moans, pants, gasps, screams and squawks, they want to appear the world's greatest lover, whereas what they really are afraid of revealing is that they are actually lukewarm about sex.

They really don't know what all the fuss is about, but feel obliged to fall in with the great popular fallacy that all orgasms must be earth-shattering sensations and sex has to be lustily noisy.

Female fakers tell themselves a little feigning on their part boosts the quality of their male partner's performance. They figure that if they don't thrash about in apparent frenzy, their men will wonder if they are

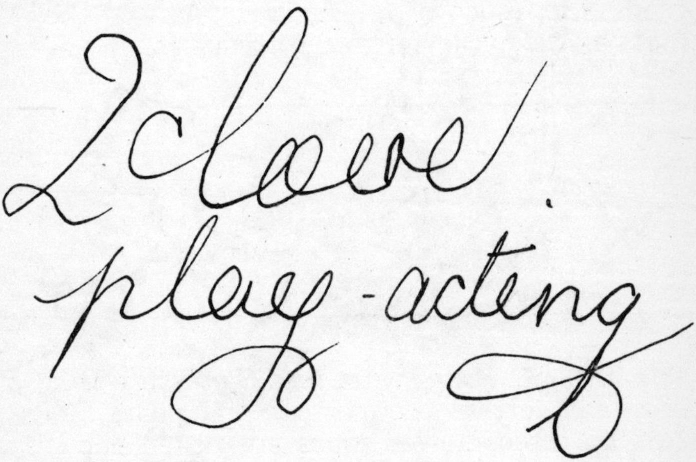

frigid, or whether their own technique is inept. Often it is, but a little make-believe play-acting is seen as preferable to a frank exchange of words on individual preference.

In time, the attainment of a perfect and undetectable faked performance becomes the prime goal over even personal satisfaction. The thrill comes from the acting, not the act.

Men, too, can be fakers, and their motive is to appear as a tiger, even if in reality and by inclination they are mere neutered toms.

The size of the Fakers' writing is enormous and it is peppered with extravagant flourishes. Lower zones are balloon-like. The writing has a right slant and is full. Some letters are disconnected.

Easy Lays

It's hard to be good, but it requires no effort to be easy.

Easy lays don't believe in formal introductions, hand-

Easy lays don't believe in formal introductions.

picked partners or deep emotional tangles. They love the spontaneity of sex without strings, whenever and wherever they fancy it.

Pick-ups and pushovers are their stock-in-trade. Orgies and one-night-stands are a real rave with no repercussions.

Plentiful sex with a different partner plucked off the sexual merry-go-round whenever the music stops is their aim to combat boredom and the frightening prospect of emotional responsibility.

Female Easy Lays enjoy the role of object of any man's desires. Even a stranger's arms around her in the wee small hours will banish loneliness. And she enjoys an extra kick from anonymous sex. Without the embarrassment of getting to know the procession of men in her life as individuals, she can let herself go, bending over backwards to give a memorable unhibited performance to each and every one.

Male Easy Lays are just as cynical and clinical about what they want.

Easy come, easy go ...

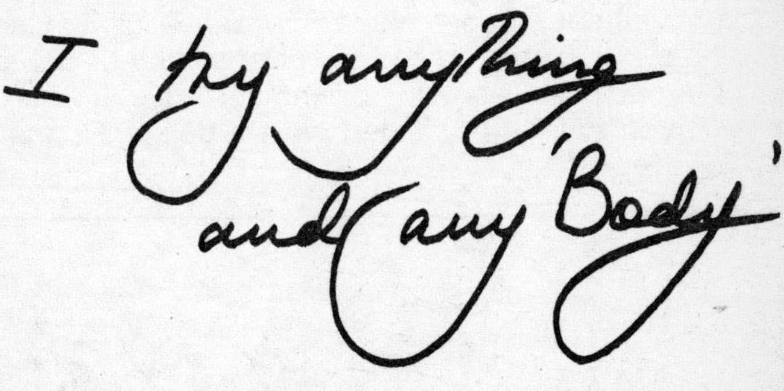

Easy Lays can be right or left slanters. The writing is very pasty and irregular. Broad letters and arcades are featured, and lower zones are rounded.

The Selective

The Selective seek a pure-bred pedigree partner, and are every bit as critical and discriminating as a judge at Crufts Dog Show.

Clannish and particular about the company they keep, they ruthlessly root out mongrels and rank-outsiders as undesirables and insist on the highest standards from their own kind.

With such strong expectations, they know they will never find the partner they seek from chance encounters with strays down dark alleys. Any unwelcome sniff of interest or approach is treated with disdain. They reveal themselves only to the chosen few in private showings which are always exclusive and secret, as the Selective feel safe only in the company of their own caste or class.

Closed clubs, secret societies and cliques that feature rituals, ceremonies or even sorcery appeal to them, as they admit only an exclusive few.

The Selective expect others to mind their own business and never feel the need to reveal their own intimate data to the riff-raff.

Even if their search for a partner is a long and lonely one, they will not compromise their standards. Expect to be checked out from top to tail for any flaw or defect if you come under the scrutiny of the Selective. If you pass the test, you will be rewarded with a doggedly clannish lover for life.

I only fancy a few

The Selective use distinct pressure. Writing is upright with a slight tendency to lean to the left. Wide margins and wide spaces are made between words. The writing looks angular and lower zones extend to the left.

Erotic Fantasists

Reality may be lying in bed with the bills due, a streaming cold, a screaming child in the next room, and a partner who is snoring lifelessly.

But with a flick of the magic switch located in the brain, the fantasy reels start rolling. Like a private view of a porno movie, fantasy floods all the senses with powerful erotic evocations of favourite sexy scenarios, including personal remakes of all the well-known fairy tales featuring Sleeping Beauty aroused with a passionate kiss, to Cinderella with all Buttons undone.

Taking the starring part in the action, our female Fantasist is the seductive social climber who puts the sin in Cinderella, or Snow White driven to the depths and heights of passion by the Prince. All the power and the glory, the tense and searing bodice-ripping, shuddering lust that seems to be missing from real life in Dollis Hill or Knotty Ash comes alive in her dreams.

Our male Fantasist carries on where James Bond and delicacy left off. He just has to spy a woman who stirs his curiosity and his sexual antennae to swing into action mentally as a macho rampant Rambo substituting laying for slaying. The women, all curvaceous and sexually smouldering, are left breathless with lust after each encounter, conquered by his irresistible looks, his incredible staying power, his stylish and practised performance and the mocking urbanity of his wit and intelligence.

The desires of all Fantasists are actually full-blooded and earthy. They just need a hefty injection of fantasy to help their bodies accept mediocre and disappointing reality, like the sugar-coating on a very bitter pill.

Erotic Fantasists' writing can be all slants and all styles. Its prime feature are the exaggerated loops in the lower zone. Capitals are full and letters are broad.

Pious Prudes

Pious, pompous and pontificating (and sounding like a firm of Spanish Inquisition lawyers), the Prudes love telling the world that sex is shameful, our bodies are possessed by devilish urges, and illicit lust will be punished by eternal damnation.

Pleasures of the flesh are denounced as wickedness that should be stamped out, leaving the body pure and chaste. By renouncing sexual gratification they believe they cleanse the soul like a miracle biological washing powder. By sacrificing sexual satisfaction they trust they will stiffen their moral fibre.

Abstinence at all times and a strict avoidance of temptation is the creed they follow, and they can't resist climbing on their soap boxes and preaching the path of righteousness to others.

The Pious Prudes recycle their own natural urges into crusading efforts to save the human race from an unwholesome and unholy fall from grace.

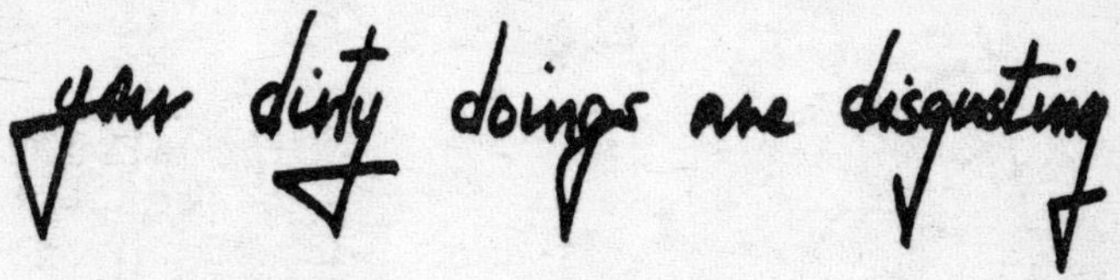

The Prude's writing is sharp and angular. The upper zone is very tall, the middle zone compressed. Heavy pressure is used on single downstrokes and horizontal movements. Lower zones are pointed with triangle formations.

Fickle Heartbreakers

Love 'em and leave 'em is the philosophy of the Fickle. They blow hot and cold emotionally, inflamed with consuming desire one minute, then cooling off rapidly to move on to another conquest.

Responsibility for other people's happiness is considered a lumber they can do without. Clinging vines are ripped up by the roots and left lovelorn, limp and unsupported in their wake.

New thrills and sensations are the aphrodisiac they seek to feed their restlessness. Charm and affability make victims fall in flocks at their feet. The more resistance

The Fickle are freelancers, born to rove and wander.

met, the harder they try as they need to get their own way at all costs. Underhand or cruel means can be used if thwarted in their attempts to weaken by dependence and then control others.

Fickle Heartbreakers have an uncanny adaptability which is part of their spell. They can feign helplessness and behave like an infant to arouse interest. Swearing eternal love and denying that they will ever leave, they also know how to lie and deceive.

While it lasts, a Fickle Heartbreaker gives their lover the million-dollar treatment. Attentive, generous, entertaining and clever, nobody does it better. They are champions at the game and ensure they make such an impact no one else will be able to assuage or massage the broken heart they have left behind.

No one can cope with them or capture them. They won't be tied down with commitments, emotional strings or caring considerations. The Fickle are freelancers born to rove and wander.

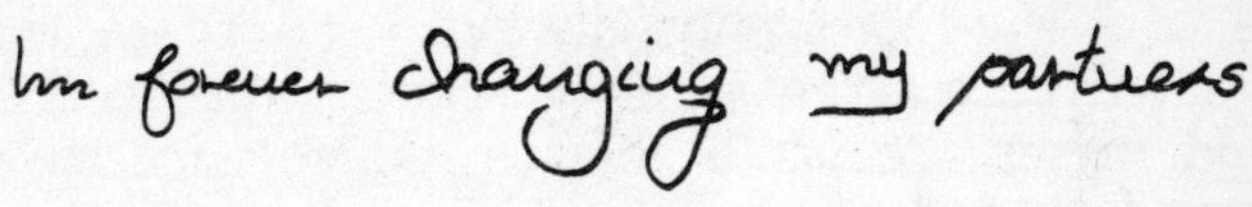

Fickle Heartbreakers' writing is large, broad and with mixed slant in the middle zone. There is a variety of lower zone formations. Exaggerated capitals, garlands and elaborated letters produce an irregular flow. The lines are wavy.

Drama Merchants

If Drama Merchants ever needed patron saints, John McEnroe and Tatum O'Neal reportedly fit the bill with their controversial screamings and screechings.

Drama Merchants' lives are a daily drama. Something always happens to cause uproar, and if it doesn't happen naturally, they provoke it.

Temperamental and easily upset, the slightest incident sends them over the edge. Even in the lulls before the storm, they heave and sigh excitedly and never fail to make their presence felt.

Loud and shrill of voice, their clothes, expressions and gestures stand out in a crowd to ensure they are never ignored.

Romantic relationships with Drama Merchants are

always turbulent, as any emotional overload causes them to turn even an intimate moment into chaos.

Their hyped-up energy inevitably spills over into the bedroom scene. They expect the earth to move for them. But if it doesn't, the outcry is enormous.

They fight with their lovers like dragons, with nostrils aflare and scales aquiver. Any soap opera or tragedy, but especially their own, is the signal for a free flow of tears. Like any stage-struck ham actor, they know that their terrible over-the-top scenes always keep them in the spotlight with the attention they feel they deserve. Even boos and hisses are preferable to indifference to keep their egos fully fed.

Drama Merchants use heavy pressure and form large loops everywhere. Writing may slant three ways. The letters are very broad, the capitals gigantic and spacing between words is irregular.

Dressers

While most people undress for sex, Dressers like to put on their favourite outfits to suit the occasion. Birthday suits are definitely out.

Uniforms of all forms stimulate their sexual imagination from nurses' gear to French maid's frillies or full Hitler regalia.

While most people undress for sex, Dressers like to put on their favourite outfits.

Rubber clinging tightly and hotly, leather smacking of unyielding strength and power, and sensuous materials like silk, fur, satin and chiffon tease and excite more than bare skin ever can.

Keeping on the wrappers adds an air of mystery and suspense that Dressers love. Getting into gear for sex enhances their exhilaration and excitement, proving that anticipation really is nine-tenths of the pleasure.

Nudity makes them feel vulnerable by comparison and shrinks their sexuality. Wearing the armour provided by clothes bolsters their confidence, unleashes their libidos and spices their fantasies. Looking good signals feeling good.

Dressers have ornate writing with bizarre, artificial shapes, covering strokes, distorted lower zones, and wide spacing between the lines. The upper zones look distorted and cracked. Writing slants to the left.

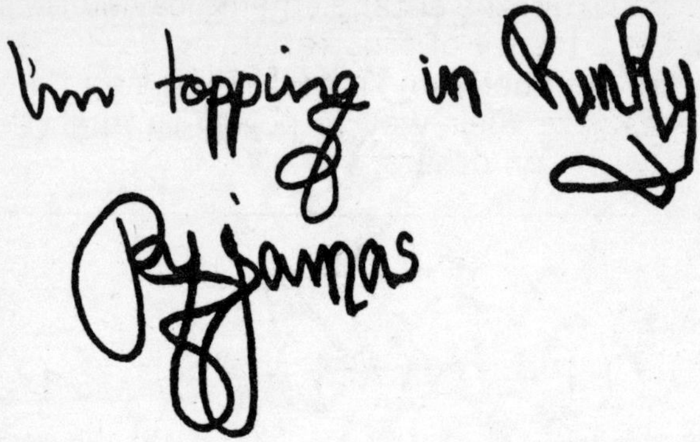

Teasers

Teasers are sexual spiders who catch their prey in their web.

Wily, artful, persistent, credible and cunning, they tantalize and titillate until they have led their trusting victims all the way up the garden path. It leads nowhere.

Teasers spin a shining gossamer web of faith, hope and flattery. Then they set about luring their innocent victim into it. An elaborate seduction ritual takes place, using charm, wit, innuendo, whispers, smouldering looks, caresses and suggestions until they have bedazzled and completely captured and cornered their quarry.

Once the emotional trap has been sprung, the Teasers' prey are helpless but to fall into it and succumb.

At this point, Teasers are adept at reassuring their victim. Displays of affection and interest are redoubled, tireless and convincing. Once hearts have been won, Teasers have the power they seek. Their influence is total as they tickle and tease, soothe and spoil, stoking the flames of passion in their partner.

Not until their prey are completely compliant and panting, powerless and pleading – it's called Crunch Time

– will Teasers deliver the *coup de grâce.* That is when they wriggle free from the entanglement, leaving their victims stranded in a frenzy of frustration.

Teasers get their fun from cliff-hanging flings where they manipulate their way to power through the sexual hold they exert on others.

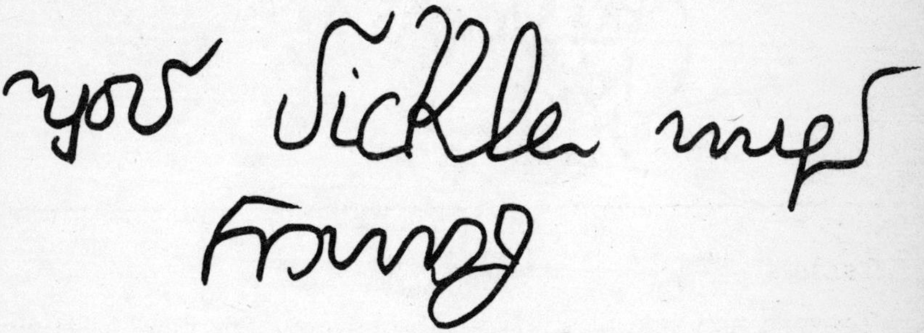

Teasers' writing slants to the right. The middle zone is large but the lower zone stumpy. Writing size is medium. It features ticks on the upper zone letters.

Applause Junkies (or Was My Performance the Best?)

Few perform better than Applause Junkies. Practice has made perfect and their style and panache marks them down as sexual sophisticates.

Sex is regarded by them as no haphazard tumble but a star performance that needs serious preparation to keep in peak condition. Their bodies are pampered and trim and presented as hygienically as an oven-ready turkey.

No matter what other walks of life they have found distinction in, their sexual rating is the one that gives them greatest satisfaction – and anxiety. Having passed the initial grades with honour they are anxious to keep up the standard that draws the praise they crave.

Male Applause Junkies know they are hunky and

... a fragile ego ...

handsome, but are determined to prove that they are the most proficient at using their equipment.

Female Applause Junkies know that whatever their age, they look a knockout. But they need constant reassurance that their allure hasn't slipped or the old magic hasn't started to wear off.

Applause Junkies have to be told exactly how they have scored after every sexual session. Being true perfectionists they insist on critical appraisals. It has to be top marks or a standing ovation every time, as anything less will depress them for days.

Beneath that confident, accomplished façade there is actually a fragile ego that needs to be boosted by incessant and exaggerated reassurance.

Applause Junkies love to use spirals at the beginnings of words. The writing has a left slant and is large. D's and t's are looped and in the lower zone, double loops are used. Dots on the i are circular. The end of the first capital is

extended to run under the rest of the words. Personal initials are especially large. Rounded tops can be seen on m's and n's.

D-I-Y Lovers

Self-sufficiency rules, OK? When it comes to releasing and relieving sexual tension, D-I-Y lovers need no help. Nobody does it better than they do.

Fastidious in their habits, D-I-Y lovers are secretive about their private pleasure sessions. They are good customers for magazines and books that fire their desire and lock themselves away to leaf through them in solitary splendour.

Masturbation is safe, convenient and satisfying and does not risk emotional involvement that can produce pain, rejection and responsibility. D-I-Y lovers face no competition, need spend no money on seduction and know there is only one winner past the finishing post – them.

D-I-Y lovers are good customers for magazines and books that fire their desire

Forming intimate partnerships presents problems, the prime one of which is communicating sexual need which D-I-Y merchants find embarrassing. It is also frustrating to have to bother making anyone else happy when pleasing yourself is so much easier and simpler.

I flog myself to death

D-I-Y lovers have backward slanting tendencies. The 'o' at the end of words as in 'to' and 'do' curls around to cover the top. The letter 'a' is inverted. Concealing strokes are made to letters and wide gaps are left between words and lines to indicate a wish to seek seclusion.

Gentlemen

Gentlemen don't have cold feet or cold hands, rough manners or rough language.

They handle every woman as if she were the most fragile and fascinating object ever encountered.

A Gentleman's bed manners are impeccable.

Gentlemen are tender. As sex siren Marlene Dietrich said of Ernest Hemingway, the man who modelled the original macho label: 'He was gentle, as all real men are gentle; without tenderness a man is uninteresting.'

A Gentleman's bed manners are impeccable. Thoughtful, chivalrous and graceful, he makes lovemaking an effortless art that he can perform with ease, style and delicacy. There are no rough edges to his actions or attitudes. Timing is slow and deliberate and control, courtesy and consideration are crucial to him. No matter how hot his feelings, he can keep his passion on a back burner until his partner starts to come to the boil.

Sympathetic and empathetic, a gentleman cares about his performance and his ability to give pleasure. They are a very rare breed.

Patient, practised and always in peak condition, a gentleman never pounces. His own needs are requested politely. And when it's all over, a gentleman will always make sure he hasn't hogged more than his fair share of the duvet.

If you ever come across one, wrap him in a plain brown envelope and post him to me.

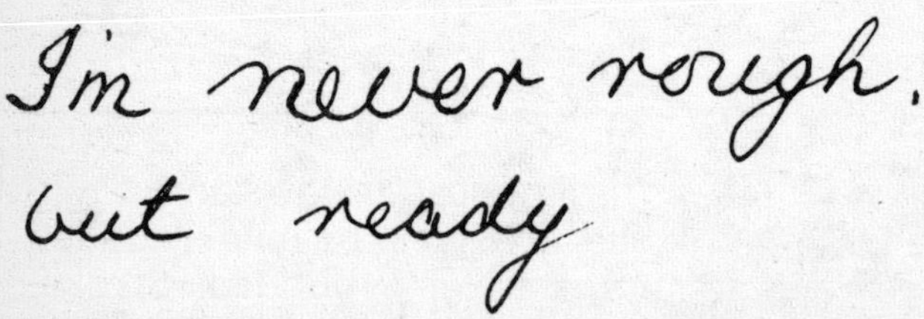

Gentlemen use copybook style. Loops are completed and many starting strokes are used. Writing never grows larger than medium at the most. The slant is to the right.

Cuddlers and Caressers

Outgoing and demonstrative, Cuddlers are human hugging machines. They need plenty of affection plus body contact from petting, pinching, touching and stroking.

Over-familiarity with even strangers drives them to stand closer to contacts than normal intimate interaction allows. Cuddlers are 'space invaders', inching closer than most people find comfortable. Fondling foreplay is their favourite turn-on. The more daring will rub a tantalizing hand secretly and discreetly under a dinner party table, their target an unsuspecting guest opposite.

Cuddlers suffer from skin hunger, a chronic craving for a warm contact that only a hefty helping of hugging can cure. A cuddle provides the comforting emotional reassurance they need, and from that springs a sexual arousal, although not all Cuddlers and Caressers see the sex act as the primary object of touching and being touched.

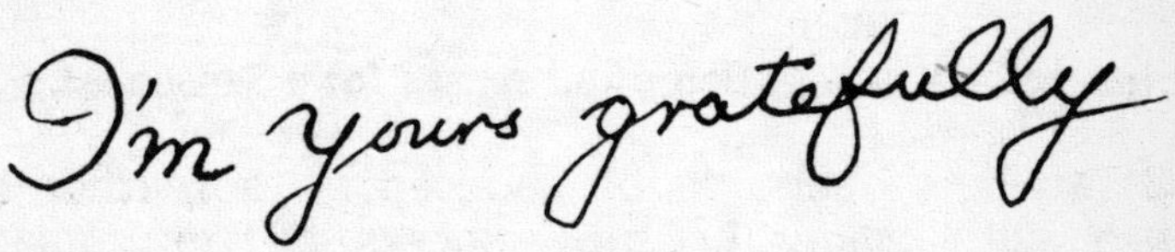

Cuddlers have a pronounced right-slanted writing. Lower and upper loops are well formed rounded and completed, and letters are very rounded. Strokes are thick.

Sensualists

Sex has to be a celebration of all senses for a Sensualist.

Sight, sound, touch, smell and taste have to be satisfied in a riot of eroticism.

Sex has to be a celebration of all senses for a Sensualist.

Sensualists yearn to be seduced on a feather bed draped with silken or satin sheets or fur rugs, or stretched naked on a sun-drenched sandy beach or a cool fern forest floor. To fill their nostrils with heady scents, their ears with low and vibrant romantic or insistent music and their bellies with fine wine and food lights the touchpaper that fires their passion.

Voluptuousness and full-blown endowments are a definite turn-on. The Sensualist is sharply aware of body odour, powerful perfume and shapes and forms that resemble body contours, especially breast and buttock-shaped ones.

The Male Sensualist laps up the sights and sounds that

smack of earthy Eastern promise, especially strippers or belly dancers whose hot and sultry suggestive movements, thinly veiled and covered, signal sexual innuendo.

The Female Sensualist spends more time than the average woman pampering and preening, adorning and grooming with expensive treatments, lotions and potions to make her body soft and appealing to touch, sight and smell.

Massage is irresistible to Sensualists of both sexes.

Self-indulgent and hedonistic joyous pleasures are their goals through life. As wrinkly OAPs they still enjoy the contact that sparks that twinkle in their eyes, even as the nurse rubs their chest with wintergreen ointment.

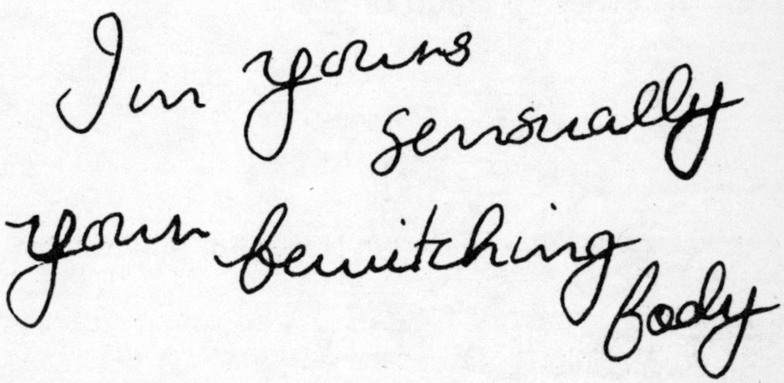

Sensualists use medium pressure and slant moderately to the right. The baseline formations are rounded and letters are partially disconnected. Beginning strokes are used, as well as scented notepaper. The lines rise.

Jokers

Sex is an unending source of laughs for Jokers. It's one big belly laugh, from the ridiculous positions it puts participants in to the peripheral fund of jokes it spawns on the fringes.

Full of fun and never far from playing the fool, Jokers find bedtime a riot. There are no fixed hours or rules and there is always a comical twist, observation or comment to exploit to the full.

A little laugh relieves the tension and anxiety that can inhibit sexual expression, which is why apple pie beds appeal to practical jokers. But never knowing where to draw the line, they can stun their audience of one by their buffoonery and childishness, from distractions as dramatic as itching powder to whoopee pillows and plastic doggy piles. At critical moments they pull a cracker and shout hooray.

Shock is the Jokers' stock-in-trade, leaving partners uncertain whether to laugh or cry.

Sex is an unending source of laughs for jokers.

Giggles and tickles can always diffuse serious moments of passion, fizzling it out to slapstick.

Not all Jokers are as harmless as they seem, as a thin veil of merciless cruelty can be present, though masked, in some personal practical jokes.

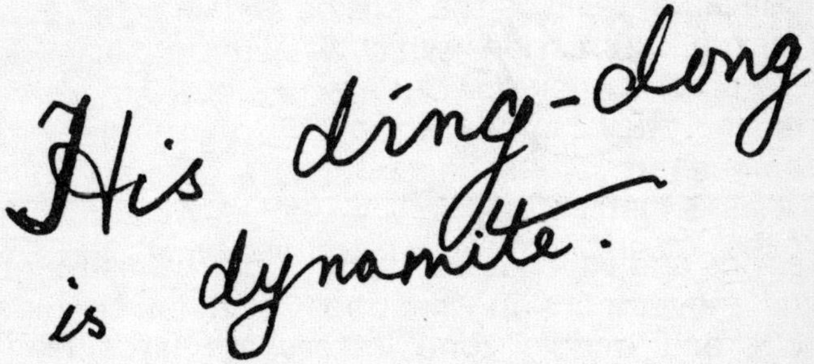

Jokers have wild, large writing, which moves in three directions. Adornments to letters are added, and upper zone and lower zones show exaggerated extensions. The letter 'n' has a quick turn up on the end stroke. The 't' bars have horsewhip crosses. The lines soar upwards.

Weirdos and Psychos

Weirdos and Psychos get their kicks from their kinks. Those who equate pleasure with pain turn on to thrashings and punishments, humilation and domination.

These strange bedfellows find hurt sharpens their sensations – whether they are on the receiving end or administering it. Straight sex rarely appeals and props are invariably essential for their practices.

The key to their perverted persuasions is power which has become distorted into an abnormal sexual contact.

Birds of this particular feather tend to flock and flog together.

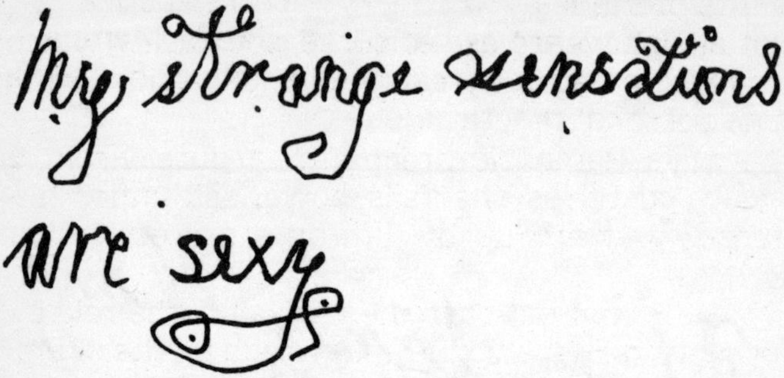

Weirdos and Psychos add bizarre flourishes to letters. Unusual movements in the upper and lower zone are apparent and middle zone letters are large lean and twisted. The baseline is irregular and dips. A mixture of arcades and angles are used. Dots and spots appear in unorthodox positions.

Romantics

Romantics need a regular injection of pulse-racing, sweet-talking, tear-jerking, knee-weakening, heart-stopping emotion to stoke the romantic content of their humdrum lives.

Being in love – and mourning lost love – is an essential state, with all its sighing, day-dreaming, yearning and searing sexual electricity.

Crazily veering from happy hype to heartbreak, their sentimental bucket is so full it overflows at the mention of anyone else's sob stories or unrequited love tangles.

Romantics find comfort and soaring inspiration from poetry and satisfaction from pouring out their feelings in love letters, secret notes and doodles. They find significance in snatches of haunting music, feel sentimental about souvenirs and photographs and nostalgic for places that have been the locations for romantic interludes.

Romantics wear rose-coloured spectacles which blur the raw rough edges of reality, giving idealized images of their lovers.

The Male Romantic dreams of a pure virgin whose petticoats rustle as she falls powerless under his spell before being swept up by him on a protective wave of tenderness.

Female Romantics cast themselves in the role beloved of true love trash magazines, featuring all the old familiar clichéd situations, from moonlit beaches to dancing under the stars in the arms of a handsome hero.

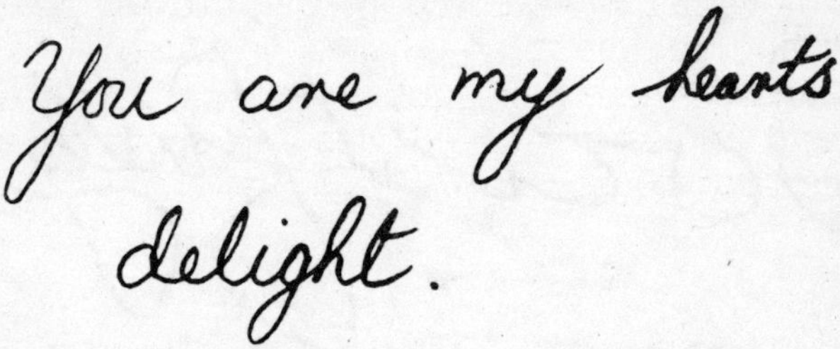

Romantics have a marked right slant with orthodox loops in both upper and lower zones. Strokes are slightly thin. They use a carefully written and conventional writing style with rounded end strokes.

Kiss-and-Tellers

Bedroom blabbermouths get more fun from kissing-and-telling than they do from the sexual act. In a compulsion to hang all their dirty laundry on the line in full view, facts get blown up to larger-than-life proportions and intimate secrets get a thorough public airing.

No detail is spared in the verbal action-replay

afterward. Locations, durations and permutations are laid on the line to the world at large.

Loquacious salaciousness gives them status with their friends and colleagues, neighbours or drinking companions. Fuelling the gossip grapevine and being the top topic of the public announcement system gives them notoriety and the satisfaction of a wider audience for their activities.

Slightly dishonest and definitely disloyal, Kiss-and-Tellers will always swear to their lovers that their lips are sealed, even while booking air-time on local radio to broadcast their latest crowing conquests.

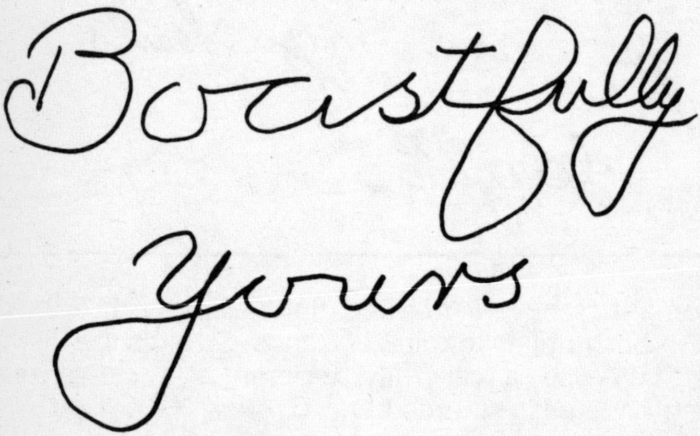

Kiss and Tellers' writing is big and flamboyant and loops are overblown. The wide and pasty style features broad middle zone formations. Letters in the middle zone are left open on the top and to the left side.

Brutes and Bone-Crushers

Trained at the King Kong School of Gentle Seduction, Brutes and Bone-Crushers make love with the delicacy of an axe.

While they may not actually beat either their chests or their partners into submission, Brutes and Bone-Crushers would probably be better paired off with an indestructable rubber blow-up doll than a real partner.

Powerful and insensitive, they thrash about and throw their weight around in the throes of passion. They bracket manliness with brute force and have no truck with consideration, foreplay or tenderness. If questioned, they will justify their brutishness by declaring that all

Powerful and insensitive...

women secretly want to be submissive and enjoy a bit of rough stuff.

Black and blue bruises, the inevitable result of a bout with a Bone-Crusher, are seen as a badge of honour, not a shameful indictment of misapplied strength.

They are the product of childhood conditioning, brought up in an environment where physical strength not mental agility were traded in the labour pool. They also experienced violence as children as a form of behaviour control.

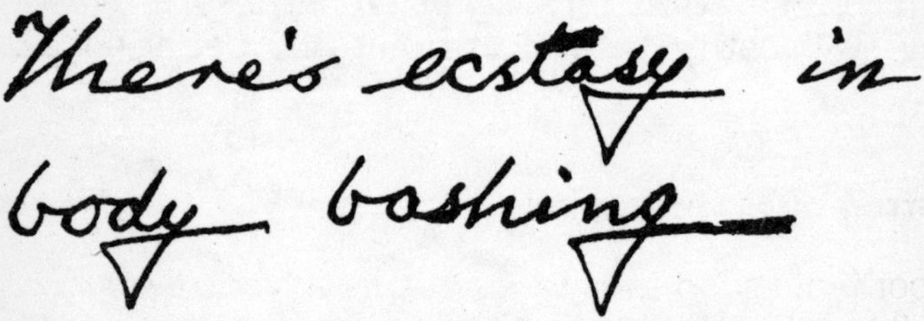

Brutes and Bone-Crushers use very heavy pressure which increases on end strokes. They may even stab into the paper with their pens. An extreme right slant and angular style features webbed feet formations in lower zone.

Poor Little Rich Girl

This is one bored broad.

Living in a palatial pad with hot and cold running servants, she is the mistress of all she surveys and has everything in life anyone could want – looks, loot, luxury, class, comfort.

Seldom bothered by the demands of married life and faced with aristocratic indifference from her jet-hopping husband, the commodities she enjoys in plenty are time,

Mistress of all she surveys...

opportunity and money for sexual adventures.

It is amusing to her to taunt the male hired help with unexpected glimpses of nudity. It is the merest dalliance to lead the young and susceptible staff on a sexual goose-chase, goading them into straying on dangerous ground.

Cocooned in her gilded cage, she likes to break out by

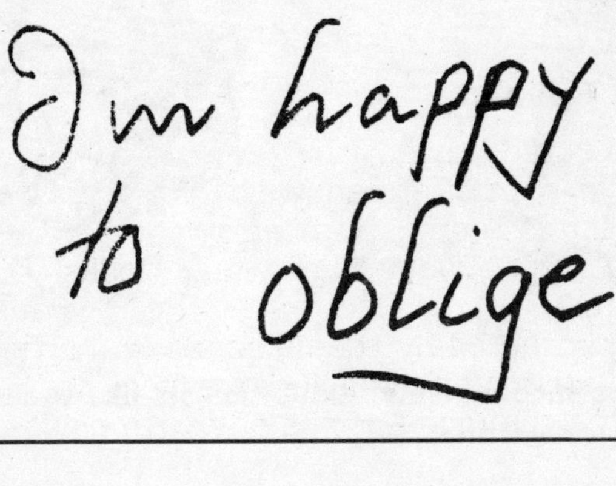

crossing the shock barrier. Her own discreet personal procurer finds the men she really enjoys and at the right price. Well-built, rough, uncultured, simple and as close to nature as possible, they provide exactly what she wants: raw, unsophisticated sex.

Within her own social circles, she is the upper-class lady with perfect airs and graces. When she leaps over the great class divide, she revels in the role of tramp.

The Poor Little Rich Girl leaves a wide left margin. The writing looks slightly blotchy and the lettering is broad. Very wide spaces are left between the words. Lower zone formations vary. The letters 'a' and 'o' are closed.

Exhibitionists

Exhibitionists love to put all their goods on display like Harrods shop window.

Surprise and shock from showing off gives them a high.

Female Exhibitionists make an elaborate ritual from undressing with the curtains open, certain that every

Like Harrods shop window, Exhibitionists like to display their goodies.

move and removal is being noticed by furtive onlookers or unwary passengers passing on the top deck of a bus. They go out of their way to climb stairs or ladders knowing that those below will enjoy the view.

The male species is the hardy breed who lurk behind park bushes or hedges and expose themselves.

Exhibitionists always try to ensure that their romps are watched by others. It heightens their excitement to know that they are putting on an erotic peepshow.

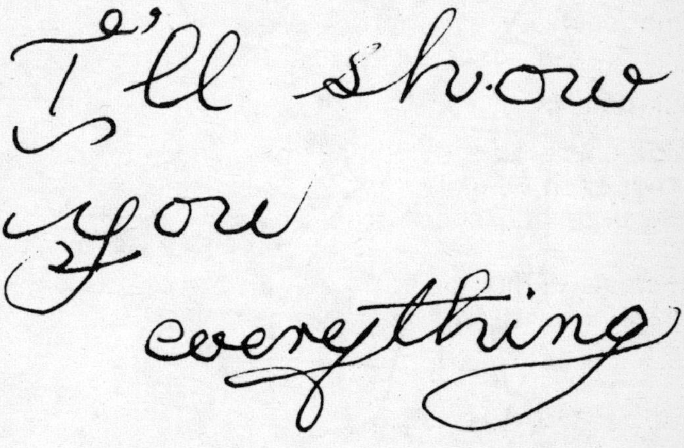

The Exhibitionists' writing is huge. The writing is broad and decorative letters are used, others are printed script, standing apart from the rest. Huge starting strokes and extensive ends extend the words.

Heavy Breathers

Phone freaks need to dial a lone impressionable woman and talk dirty to gain relief.

For the furtive Heavy Breather, there is safety in anonymous telephone numbers.

For the furtive Heavy Breather, there is safety in anonymous telephone numbers.

They dare not make personal house calls as close communication scares them. Long-distance contact via the telephone line is as near as they can cope with.

They are emboldened by the shock and fear they produce in their unknown victims, giving them a perverted twist of triumph.

The subject-matter is rarely changed, no matter how often they make the calls.

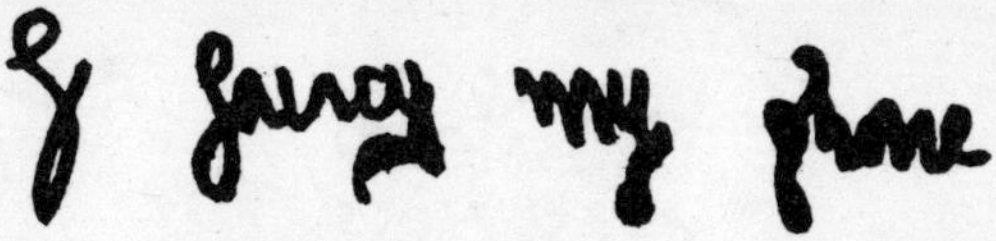

Heavy Breathers slant to the left. Their writing is small and lower loops are distorted. Pressure changes as they write. The writing is extremely connected. The 'i' dot is precisely placed and bizarre leftward openings of the middle zone can be seen. The strokes are blotchy.

Guilt-Ridden Lovers

Guilt is the skeleton that rattles in their conscience cupboard, haunting them whenever sex stirs their feelings. Overburdened by guilt from the past, they find it difficult to live for the day or welcome the future.

Their natural urges are just as strong as anyone else's but full satisfaction is blocked by the anxieties that seep into their guilt-racked minds. Regrets and recriminations of past experiences stray into their current relationships and screw up their responses.

Over-zealous mothers who put strong emphasis on punishment for forbidden sexual exploration plant the idea in childhood that sex spawns guilty and wretched feelings. Impossibly high standards of moral behaviour were set, with no allowance made for human weakness.

Sexual lapses in later life lead to exaggerated feelings of guilt that are difficult to assuage.

Guilt-Ridden Lovers have small middle zone and long upper and lower zones. There is a leftward lean to lower loops. Basically the handwriting slants to the right with some leftward bowing movements. The writing looks

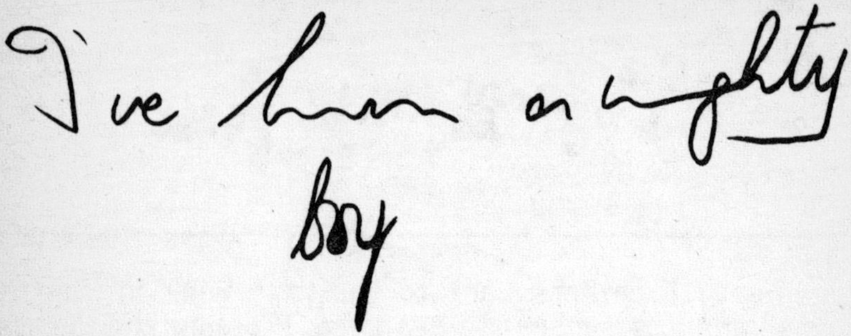

smeary, dishevelled and shaky, even disguised. The lines droop.

Compatibility

Mr Chalk and Miss Cheese

The sexually unsuitable are inexplicably drawn to each other, like north and south poles of magnets.

Strongly attracted and just as fiercely repelled by each other, their fights are fuelled with impatience and intolerance. East–West politics seem peaceful and compatible by comparison.

Mr Chalk and Miss Cheese hate being drawn to each other, but they can't kick the habit. Bed is a battlefield of power struggles and score-settling. Anger, pride, stubbornness and revenge mixed with passion tick away in an emotional timebomb that is triggered off when the sexual fire is lit.

Compatible Pairs

Life rolls on smoothly, with no earthquakes, thunderstorms or grey clouds to cast a shadow on cosily compatible couples. They go together like bookends, with similar tastes, thoughts, opinions, interests and sexual needs.

Compatible couples go together like bookends.

Their relationship becomes a comfortable habit that is predictable and mutually enjoyable. They know each other's responses, happily share responsibilities and financial obligations and rarely row as they seldom disagree on any issue.

They are plateau people who do not experience the peaks and troughs of emotion.

Compatible Lovers show a similarity of overall writing style with matching loops or lower zone movements.

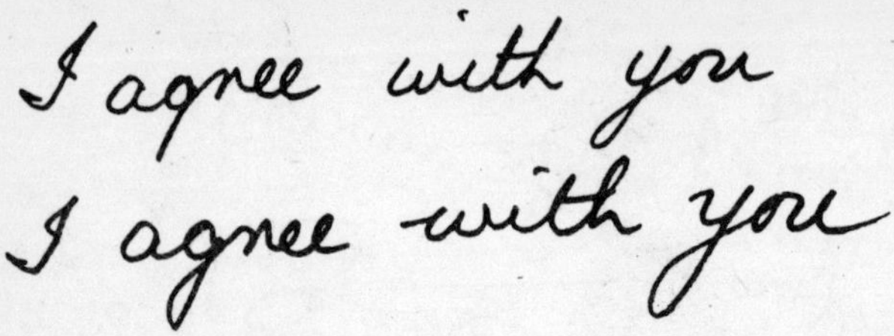

COMPATIBLE

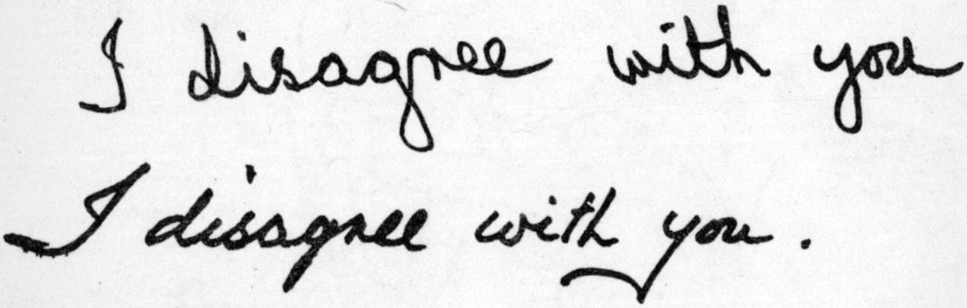

INCOMPATIBLE

Incompatible Lovers show a distinct dissimilarity of style with opposing lower zones.

Keyhole Kates and Peeping Toms

Always on the outside looking in, voyeuristic Keyhole Kates and Peeping Toms see sex as a spectator sport.

They prefer to watch and listen unobserved from the sidelines, hidden under cover of dark, concealed behind bushes, from vantage points in wardrobes or through cracks or holes in walls.

Stealthy and unobtrusive, they are closed, complicated, private characters who never let on about themselves or give much away. Like the three monkeys, they see everything, hear everything yet say nothing.

They live in a little world all of their own, shunning

Keyhole Kates and Peeping Toms see sex as a spectator sport.

society generally, especially big groups or vulgar public places of entertainment like strip joints or blue cabaret.

Peeping Toms and Keyhole Kates enjoy their pleasures in private, haunting out-of-the-way parks, heaths and lovers' lanes. But they can also get their kicks with the collusion of a partner who puts on a performance knowing that the silent phantom hidden nearby is enjoying every sigh and movement.

Being an onlooker means Keyhole Kates and Peeping Toms do not have to participate in the complexities of a real relationship. Pleasure without responsibility, giving nothing and gaining as much as the eye and ear can absorb, is preferable to emotional involvement.

Blessed with a strong visual sense and the ability to observe details concisely and accurately, they can translate their skills into clock or watchmaking or electronic board work where their precision is in demand.

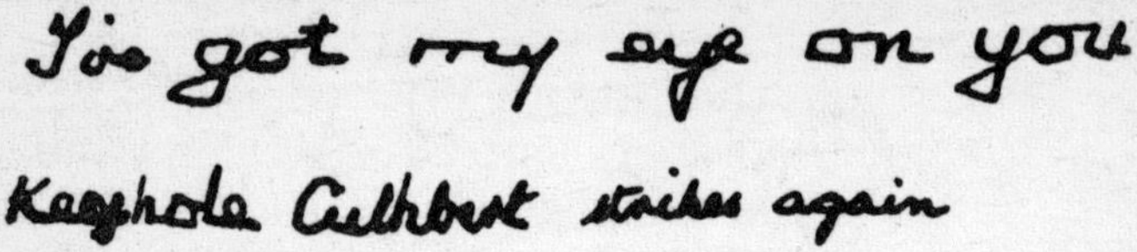

Voyeurs have microscopic writing. The 'i' dot is accurately placed and some letters have square tops. The writing is pasty and the r's have square formations. Lower loops are covered and lines fall.

Susceptible Succumbers

Susceptible Succumbers feel their sexual urges control them, not the other way around. They can be anywhere at any time, minding their own business when suddenly they are excited beyond endurance.

They are ashamed of their inappropriate feelings at inconvenient times. Women Succumbers move and squirm uncomfortably in their seats. They cannot keep their legs still, crossing and recrossing them, avoiding catching anyone's eyes. The readily aroused Male Succumber may find himself suddenly taken by storm when glimpses of something shocking in a stocking locks his mind into thoughts of sex, and no silent recitation of Latin irregular verbs or the nine-times table can rein a mind hooked on sex back to the serious business in hand.

Blushes and shameful embarrassment signal the

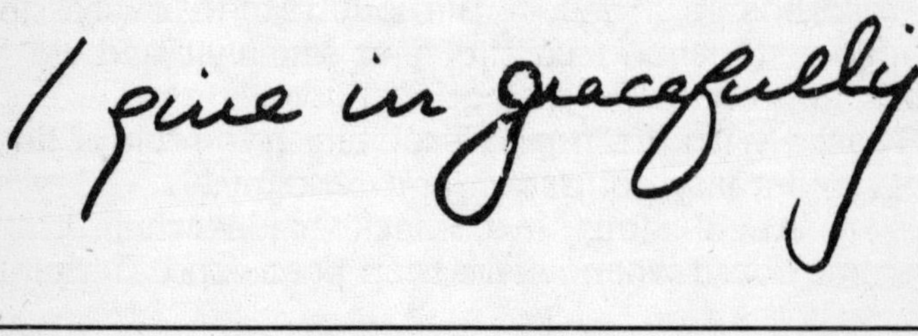

Succumbers' discomfort with their disobedient bodies. The only way out of their dilemma is to ask to be excused to seek relief from their strong drives and desires.

Susceptible Succumbers vary between long and short lower zones. There is irregular spacing of words, unequal length of upper zones and a marked right slant. The writing is pasty and irregular, the pressure is weak and garland formations can be seen in the letters.

Killjoys and Biblebashers

Killjoys can be found with their binoculars in Soho strip clubs, denouncing the disgusting spectacle unfolding before them. Killjoys wade into action in factories and offices, ripping down topless pin-ups. Killjoys frown on Christmas mistletoe capers, renounce unashamed pleasure-seekers and condemn any uninhibited display of affection.

Lust and lasciviousness can be found everywhere by the Killjoys if they look hard enough for it. And they do. Incessantly.

They speak of sex in a tight-lipped hiss, giving it the status of four-letter words like 'dirt' and 'muck'. Further clues to their view that sexual activity is nasty and not to be encouraged can be found in their campaigns, called 'crusades to clean up society'.

The Killjoys' prudish and puritanical attitudes to sex stem from their strict upbringing, with particular emphasis on rigorous potty training. Any exploration of their bodies as babies was firmly discouraged and disapproved of by their mothers. Any joyful expression or enjoyment of their sexuality and sensuality would have been punished.

Yet there is nothing like prohibition to prompt strong, secret and guilty attraction in the Killjoy.

They are obsessed with sex because their life is a struggle to control and repress and not express their own natural urges.

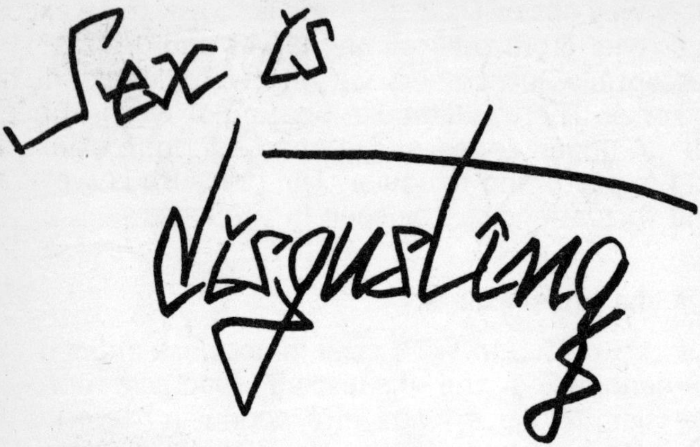

Killjoys and Biblebashers are convinced that their self-righteous attitudes should be imposed on everyone around them. And their handwriting is just as screwed up as their emotions.

Killjoys and Biblebashers show a marked right slant. Triangles are formed in the lower zones which are also twisted and stunted, and upper zones are enormous. The writing is large with heavy pressure. Ticks are put on letters and 't' bars are extra long and compulsive. The script looks blotchy.

The Fearful

Anything that smacks of sex sets off alarm bells in the brain of the Fearful.

Amorous advances trigger adrenalin of pure fear, not sex gland hormones. Saucy seductive suggestions make their knees knock and hand palms clammy.

They are not only frightened of the consequences of sex, they are fearful of their own feelings – and of failure.

To be on the safe side, they keep themselves in

Bare flesh makes them feel uneasy...

hermetically sealed impregnable packages. Their clothes are their first line of defence, from thermal underwear to tightly fastened necklines and cuffs. Even on a hot beach at the height of summer, they will wear a protective shirt or cardigan as armour plating. Bare flesh makes them feel uneasy, so they never strip off for fear of exposing themselves to looks from those around them that might contain sexual interest.

Their desires become dilemmas. Although lonely, the prospect of sexual gratification is terrifying to them, so any encouraging relationship is throttled in its infancy.

---

sexy thoughts frighten me

The Fearful end their days as timid Eleanor-Rigby-style spinsters, or crusty old batchelors.

The Fearful prefer to write on lined paper. The writing size is tiny, and the letters are cramped and narrow. The writing looks shaky and spiky. The lower zone loops are squashed stumpy and angular and triangles are formed in this erogenous zone.

Jealous Lovers

Passion and possessiveness mixed together make an explosive package of jealousy.

Immature and insecure, jealous scene-makers of both sexes are tortured by distrust.

They watch their lovers constantly for signs of betrayal and infidelity. They seethe and spit with rage at anyone at parties or social gatherings who seems to be taking a lively interest in their partner. They even glare at unknown strangers who pose a potential threat simply by proximity.

The Jealous become super-sleuths trying to catch out their partners with spot-checks. Handbags, pockets,

Handbags, pockets, wallets, even clothes are searched...

wallets, even clothes are searched for microscopic clues that prove involvement with others.

No amount of loving reassurance is ever enough. Good sex only serves as a warm-up session for an inevitable jealous interrogation, studded with accusations and taunts of past and present affairs.

In a masochistic drive to torture themselves, all the sordid details of past liaisons are demanded. Relentless questioning inevitably leads to embittered battles.

Taken to extremes, the jealous can bar unwelcome friends, workmates or even relatives from making contact. Some even try to control their lovers' clothes, hairstyles or make-up that they feel is provocative.

Jealousy always puts relationships in jeopardy, as such unreasonable behaviour drives partners into the arms of others. That is the ultimate moment of misery and triumph for the jealous, as their worst fears have then become prophetically and pathetically true.

Jealous lovers have an extreme right slant. The writing is very pasty and grasping-hooks are added to letters, as well as scrolls. The letters 't' and 'd' are looped and 'a' and 'o' are enlarged.

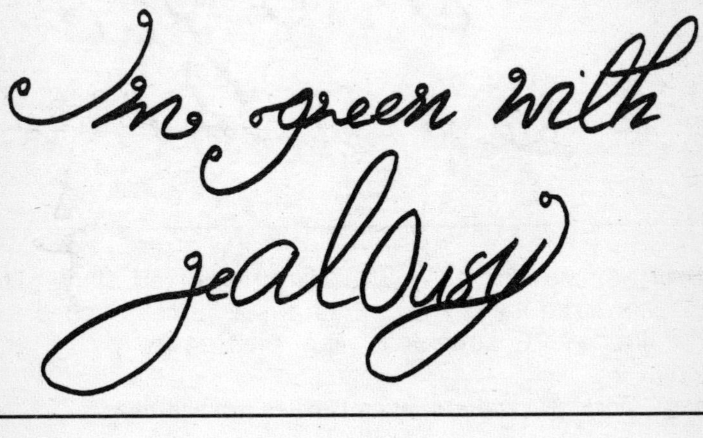

Chapter 69

The mouth is one of Mother Nature's more inspired inventions.

We use it to express ourselves, to eat and drink, to pucker up to plant kisses. We turn it down to denote displeasure and smile with it to signal sunnier feelings.

Sucking is the first accomplishment learned after a baby draws breath and becomes synonymous with pleasurable sensations, succour and security.

Lollipop lovers who prefer oral sex equate pleasure and satisfaction with the mouth.

Psychologists believe that mothers who bribed their babies to perform on the potty by giving them a dummy dipped in honey or sweeteners to soothe and comfort, establish the pattern.

As adults, the association of fulfilment and pleasure with the mouth is carried over into sexual expression.

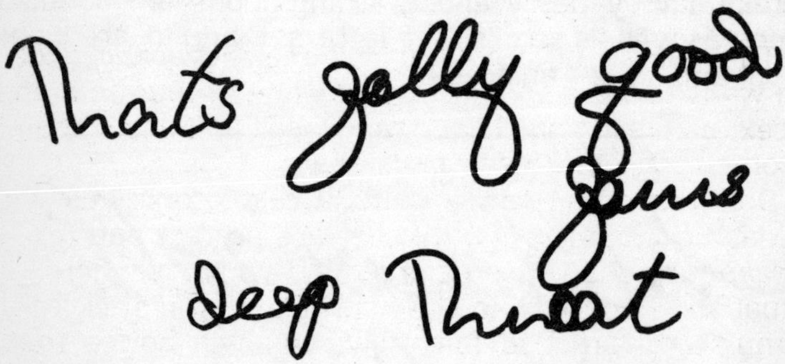

Oral Sex devotees show a varying mixed slant. The writing is irregular, with mingling of letters and lines. Lower loops are reversed. The writing is pasty and blotchy.

Chapter 3

Put to Writes – How to Become Sexier

Do you sincerely want to throw off your old hang-ups and habits and become even sexier? It is as easy as picking up a pen and practising.

Just as handwriting depicts your sexual style, it can also be used as a therapeutic tool to change your instinctive urges for the better. And it works.

All you have to do to change old negatives into exciting new positives is to write out this sentence twelve times before having sex or going to bed at night, whichever comes first.

I will practise my lower loops until I become naturally, joyfully and outrageously sexy.

This should become your revitalizing erotic ritual if you want to see a spontaneous change in your enjoyment of sex. Liberate your lower zone loops and allow them to become fuller, loopier and sexier.

Don't expect instant results. It takes conscious effort to master the strokes until they are perfect and for this to seep into your unconscious mind which is where your sexual and handwriting style springs. If you stick to this formula and practise faithfully, you will notice that it becomes easier to form the letters until in time it becomes so natural and automatic you cannot remember how you wrote instinctively before.

Then be prepared for some pleasant surprises. Personal experience is the best way to check that this simple knack works. You have nothing to lose but your inhibitions!

If you are undersexed and hold your pen near the nib, hoist up your hand to half way up the pen barrel. This will give you an earthy appetite, an artistic appreciation and resilience.

If you are debauched, depraved or degenerate, your writing will look blotchy, smudgy and smeary, with ink overflowing to fill in the lower loops, or you may retrace your loops. Hold yourpen lower down the barrel and open out your lower zone loops. This will clean up your ink strokes and clean up your thoughts, giving a more wholesome approach to sex.

If you have a low capacity for sex illustrated by sharp and spidery strokes, hold your pen higher, which will increase your libidinal urges to boost your pleasure.

Practise adding loops to your letters where there are none and put more pressure on your downstroke loops, making sure they are complete and meet back up on the baseline of the middle zone. It's not a disaster if you are loopless (so long as you avoid the irritation ticks on the end which denote impatience with your partner) but full rounded lower loops do make for more complete fulfilment.

In the upper zone, if you increase the height of letters l, h, b, t and d, you will improve your intelligence and creative fantasies. If you are a skimpy upper looper, broaden them. It will help you to lose your present inhibitions and express yourself freely emotionally.

Broad loops indicate healthy open minds.

Distorted loops (both upper and lower) indicate bizarre and twisted thinking. Iron them out for healthier emotional and sexual satisfaction.

Narrow letters indicate narrow thinking. Widen your m's, n's and u's.

Don't cramp your sexual style. Let yourself go. If your y's and g's are narrow and not fully formed and rounded upon the baseline, you are in danger of suffering from sex starvation.

If your loops dangle and tangle into the next line of writing, you are preoccupied with promiscuous thoughts of sex. Keep the lines clear and clear those tarnished thoughts at the same time.

Chapter 4

Last Writes – Love Letters and What They Reveal

If your lover's behaviour has changed towards you of late, or if you really want to know what they feel about you, look at your love letters.

They are as accurate as lie detectors to find out precisely what is going on in your closest relationships. Even a study of scribbled notes will give the game away.

If your lover is wild about you, check the way the letters of your name are written. They will pop up or stand out and grow bigger than the surrounding script if all is well, wild and wonderful. If your partner is absolutely besotted with you, the size of your name will be out of proportion to the rest of the words written. Your name may also be retraced over and over again which is their way of dwelling lovingly on thoughts of you. The capital letter of your name may well be separated from the other characters as a signal of respect to show you are special. Remember that if your lover loves you, they love your name, and show it positively in the way they write to you.

If love is cooling, the letters of your name may shrivel up or be virtually indecipherable and unreadable compared to the rest of the handwriting. Look for signs that the paper has been stabbed aggressively when writing your name, or if you are simply fading away or disappearing off the scene.

To find out how the land lies, study the writing slant used to form your name. If their normal writing is right-slanting, but your name leans back to the left, prepare to pack your bags. It means you are part of the past and they would secretly like to leave you behind, as you do not figure in their future. If their normal writing is left-slanting but your name slants to the right, they are planning ahead with you in mind, even if they have a hard time keeping up with you.

If their writing usually has a regular rhythm but goes haywire when writing your name, your lover is thoroughly mixed up about their feelings for you; loving you one moment and hating you the next. It reflects a changeable, unpredictable relationship which you can try to turn into a positive one, but it won't be easy. If their normal writing flows in three different directions yet your name is written in one even slant, it shows you are a steady influence and a source of strength to them. Stick with it.

If their writing is broad and your name is written in a cramped narrow style, there are inhibitions where you are concerned. It could be that your lover finds it difficult to open themselves up to anyone, but you need to be sure of what is being withheld and whether this is particular to you. Ask yourself, too, if you are squashing or thwarting them. If their writing is normally narrow but your name is expressed in a broad way, you are probably the only one they feel comfortable with and you refresh the parts others cannot reach. They feel happy and safe with you.

To test the temperature of your sexual attraction check the lower loops of your name. If they are large and rounded, passion is hot. If they are cut down or abruptly shortened, it indicates lukewarm feelings and a likelihood that your partner may begin to look elsewhere for sexual satisfaction.

Terms of Endearment can be checked out for the secret code they contain. How big are the kisses on the bottom and how many? You should be looking at big smackers, not narrow little pecks. In the phrase 'I love you' the word 'love' and 'you' should stand out from the others. If it droops despondently you know feelings are cooling off. 'Dears' and 'darlings' should look big and bold. Look carefully at the word 'all' in 'all my love'. If it is splattered, you could be sharing with someone else.

Ink Colours are a giveaway to a writer's character and state of mind.

Royal blue shows vitality, liveliness, energy and strength. An active mind and an expansive personality are also indicated.

Black ink is chosen by a logical, organized, businesslike person. They can be prudish, pedantic, conventional to the point of old-fashioned as they uphold family ties and religious beliefs and stick to solidarity and familiarity.

Dark-blue ink is chosen by the ordinary and the matronly. Methodical and systemmatic, they are conformists and lack imagination.

Red ink shows anger, aggression, temper and even possible accident-proneness. Passion, vitality, abrasiveness, irritability – even warlike tendencies – rebelliousness, childishness, and impulsiveness are part of the red ink writer's personality.

Light-green ink shows freshness; spiritual soul-searching characters who are interested in health and beauty, herbalism, and pacifism choose this colour. It signifies tranquillity, renewal, perception and subtlety.

Dark green shows a passionate and cruel personality; egocentricity, jealousy, sharpness, stubbornness, a hard-hearted approach and greed.

Brown ink shows harshness, anxiety, worry, stinginess, tension, pessimism, introversion, morbidity, impotence, masochism, frigidity, frustration, headaches, and the Cinderella syndrome.

Putty-coloured ink or grey shows wallflower behaviour: caution, sallowness, a lack of vitality, lethargy, and dullness of thought reflecting the insignificance of the writer.

Gold ink shows materialism, clumsiness, ostentation, love of splendour, vulgarity and lack of discrimination; loudness, affectation and artificiality.

Silver ink shows objectivity, lack of warmth, sedateness, class-consciousness, acquisitiveness. Reserve, coolness and respect for status symbols is also shown.

Light blue shows detachment, maturity, serenity, sensitivity to atmospheres, but also the insipid and wishy-washy light-mindedness, weakness, and insecurity of someone who opts for the humdrum life.

Orange ink shows boldness, argumentativeness, and sensitivity. Superficiality, ruthlessness, tardiness, a sense of humour and a love of gorging; clownish behaviour, extravagance, gushiness, spiciness and changeability are also shown.

Purple or mauve ink shows vanity, narcissism, a love of luxury and comfort, flamboyance and theatricality, inner depth, secretiveness, deviousness and snobbishness. Prima donnas and those who desire to be different from the rest of the herd use purple.

Deep-pink ink shows extroversion, kindliness, scattiness, bubbliness, effervescence, a love of people, affection, happiness, lack of discipline, a radiant optimism, a romantic outlook; hot-bloodedness; a love of the body, desire, earthiness, teasing and flirtatiousness, overindulgence, sex-appeal, and unpunctuality.

Light pink is chosen by the soft and sentimental, the sweet, naive and innocent. It denotes light-headedness, plumpness and an airy-fairy, dreamy, cherubic and flighty soul.

Crimson ink shows a love of richness and everything that is royal, chivalrous, sedate, classical, ceremonial and gallant. It also shows hot-bloodedness and gluttony and sinfulness.

White ink shows freshness, purity, distinction, clarity, sensitivity, discipline and orthodoxy. Religiously fervent, natural, sincere, clean-living characters choose white. A love of sport and heat and good staying power is also denoted.

Turquoise ink shows edginess, mixed emotions, hard-heartedness, resilience, authoritativeness to the point of bossiness, inner loneliness, changeability, fickleness and eccentricity.

Yellow ink shows cowardice, chirpiness and cheerfulness, a tendency to sit on the fence; a 'Yes' man who is indecisive, superficial, contrary and does not always have the courage of his convictions.

The use of outrageously coloured paper with ill-matched ink points to an attention-seeker with inner conflict. They are also braggarts.

People who use decorated paper which shows kitsch embellishment are displaying bad taste and a love of clutter.

Perfumed paper is chosen by the sensitive and sentimental and the incurably romantic dreamer.They want to give their affections freely.

People who send letters written on scrappy bits of paper are showing inconsiderateness, a lack of respect, meanness, but they think they have a very special message for the world.

The use of lined paper is a cover-up of emotions by those who don't want to reveal too much. Conformity of thinking to the point of pedantry is shown.

Flimsy transparent paper shows someone who wants to be invisible and melt into the shadows and not be noticed. They especially don't want anyone to see right through them.

It is not just what is written but how it is written that tells the inside story, and many a plausible partner has been caught out by slips of the pen and script psychology.

Chapter 5

Handwriting Revelations: A Handful of Stars

Elton John – Rock Superstar

Elton John's amplified lower zones broadcast his earthy appetite for sex, variety and all the things money can buy – and how!

Driven by powerful unconscious forces, his inflated sexual imagination takes him on fantastic erotic carpet rides.

He's a flirt. He loves change and change again. He loves to be touched and when he is in the mood he's romantic, tender and affectionate. But he can also suddenly switch off and turn the cold shoulder.

His writing is very positive and ambitious and shows pure creative genius with the physical energy to make his ideas work.

His handwriting also underlines the dramatic showman who can't bear to be upstaged.

Don't enclose him in hot spots or night spots as Elton yearns for wide open spaces. He needs a big house with large living quarters.

His taste is lavish, ornate and showy. Opulence would impress him and although he does have good sense of style at times he goes over the top. Expensive knick-knacks would appeal, though with his tendency to accident prone clumsiness his insurance claims and repair bills could be high.

When it comes to spending money, he couples

generosity with a shrewd ability to economize and spend wisely.

Basically lively and effervescent, he has a good sense of humour but he can explode in sudden and unexpected outbursts of pure hot temper.

In his work life, he is hard-working and a hard taskmaster, expecting and demanding perfection. He has analytical and technical ability, with an eye for detail as well as artistic flair.

For a man with such a clever and penetrating mind, he can at times be surprisingly feather-brained and forgetful.

Strong intuition helps him to sound out people and situations. He is very superstitious and could enjoy dabbling in myth and magic, impressionable to folklore and old wives' tales.

Elton John

Although an extrovert, Elton actually keeps his personal cards very close to his chest and resents those who interfere in affairs marked private.

Health weaknesses highlighted include digestion, past ear problems and tension in the upper shoulder and neck region of the back.

Samantha Fox – Model

Samantha Fox, sexiest topless pin-up model of them all, is actually an incurable romantic.

Like her outsize breasts, she likes everything to be on a big, lavish and brash scale ... especially when it comes to emotions.

Her heart rules her head and she either loves or hates with no half measures. She falls in love – wham! – fast and furious and finds it difficult to let go.

When upset, she cries herself to sleep. She would also cry buckets over sob stories or soap operas.

She has the imagination to produce vivid sexual thoughts, but sudden unexpected inhibition about sex is shown in her handwriting.

She really does have a bouncy, energetic personality with bags of vitality and nervous energy. She is excitable and has a strong dramatic nature. When angry, she shows it. But she prefers the friendly approach and wants to reach out with warmth. Oodles of charm help her get her own way with others.

Samantha is very ambitious and go-getting. She has good ideas and likes to be busy and active. A clear thinker, she has the ability to work hard and doesn't shirk.

She loves her role in the limelight and adores the attention her body brings. She also likes her social side, music and singing and meeting people.

When it comes to cash-consciousness, she loves the good things of life that money buys and would want to surround herself with the ornaments and trappings of wealth.

As befits someone who has made her name and fame from her body, she is interested in body contours and would be keen on keep-fit and health and beauty maintenance.

Although Mum has left her mark, Samantha is more of a Daddy's girl.

On the downbeat, she gets downhearted at times and can be a blabbermouth, putting her tiny foot right in it. Healthwise she has a tendency to sudden sporadic cramps.

Samantha **Fox**

Best of luck for 86,
All my love
Samantha Fox
xxx

Ivan Lendl – Tennis Star

Ivan Lendl is a man of volcanic emotional reactions. He either loves to distraction – or hates bitterly.

Being a romantic, his heart rules his head. He laughs and cries readily to express his feelings. His feelings influence his decisions, even if his emotions urge him to act impulsively.

His sensitivity and perception are so heightened he needs to protect himself by living an almost hermetic lifestyle.

On the sexual level, he is prepared to sacrifice his carnal appetite to cut out the emotional overload that comes with it.

When upset he tends to overreact and take criticism personally. When least expected, he can be effusive, warm and kind-hearted. In anti-social moments he feels cautious, lonely and insecure.

Intelligent and with an imaginative and inventive mind, he acquires knowledge and skills quickly and easily.

His personality is an intriguing one. He is not without his own brand of charm, yet he has an air of mystery about him. Others wonder what makes him tick.

Life is a serious business for Ivan, not altogether sure of what the future holds in store.

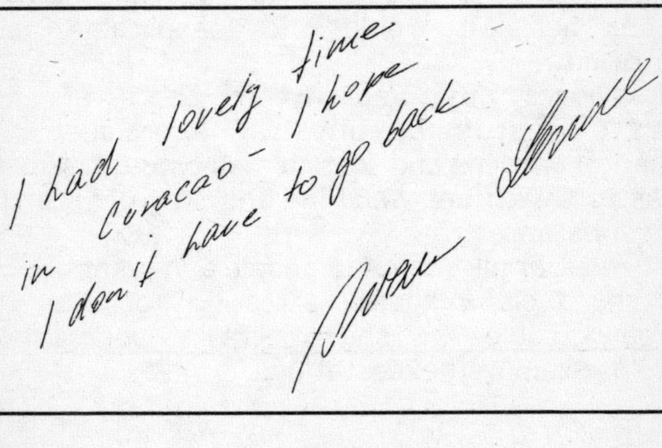

Ivan Lendl

Linda Carter – Wonder Woman

Wonder Woman Linda Carter has marvellous mental imagery and day-dreams about sex. Wild, exciting, powerful and colourful ones. This passionate woman thinks about it all the time.

She loves body contact and body language and being touched. She is emotionally charged and lives for love and romance. Tender memories and mementoes will be cherished.

Locked away in her handwriting are the painful pangs of a broken heart. She carries a torch for someone special, and finds it difficult to untie emotional knots.

Linda is very fanciful and lives in a weird and wonderful dream world which gives her a tendency to make situations larger-than-life.

Optimistic and with a good sense of teasing humour, her creative mind is a mine of bright ideas, but she is slightly scatterbrained and her thinking is sometimes woolly. Colours are vital to her and she is sensitive to atmospheres. She is very perceptive and uses her guts for guidance. Yet some of her hunches go haywire.

Her character is inwardly intricate and complicated. She can be secretive about herself and feels she is different from everyone else and very special. Psychology, the unconscious and the power of the mind would fascinate her. So would the inexplicable and the unidentified.

Linda loves music and rhythm, poetry and motion, elaborate costumes, physical exercise, animals, ornamental gardens and tropical fish would fascinate her. She has to watch her waistline and stay off starchy and sugary substances.

But most of all, she loves people and wants to be near those she feels a special affection for. She can be extremely gullible when she expects the world to come up to her rose-coloured expectations.

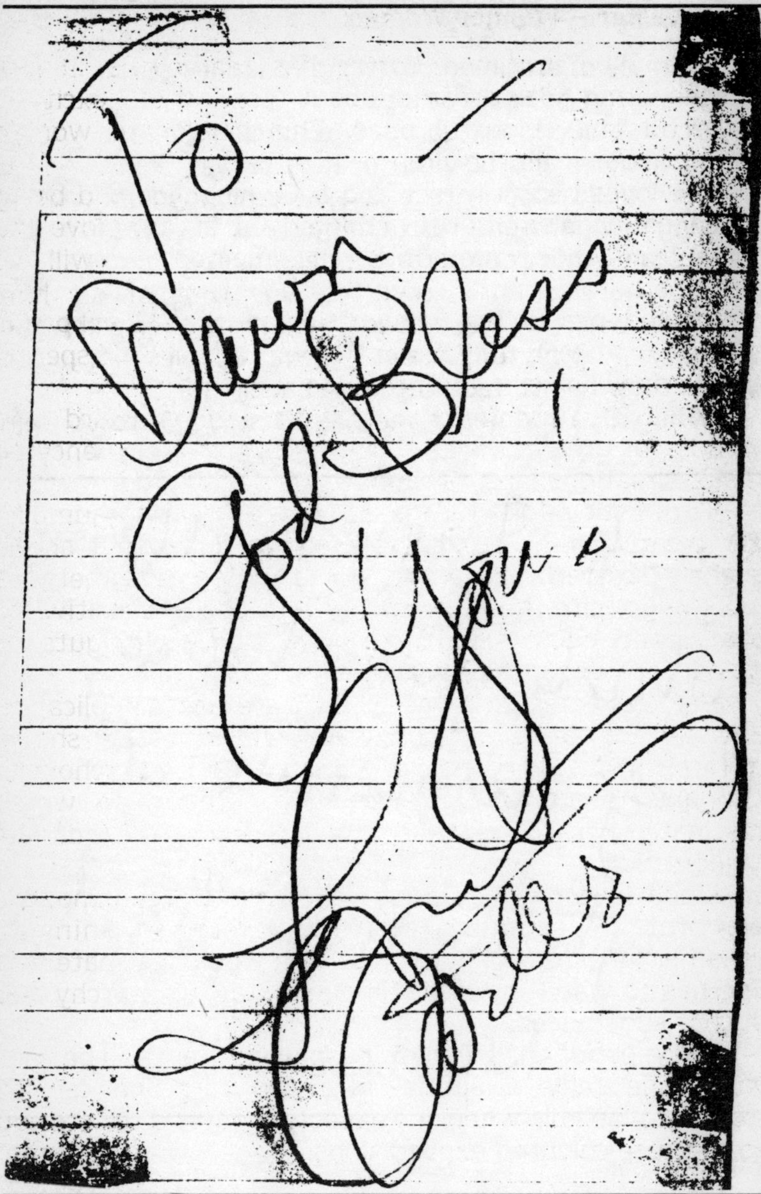

Linda Carter

Spike Milligan – Comic

Wild and vivid, erotic and exciting fantasies stir from the creative brain of Spike Milligan.

Broad-minded, outgoing and optimistic, he enjoys taking chances and playing for high stakes.

The public side is the lively comic genius who is amusing company and full of zany ideas. He likes life on a grand scale – big rooms for his personality.

But there is an introverted side that makes him withdraw when feeling at odds with himself or when the heat is on. Playing for time in this way enables him to get his act together to face the world again.

In negative moments, he has to struggle to contain

Such thing – theres
which we have
they dismantle it
anyhow we had
with Madras

Spike Milligan

himself from feelings of fury welling up inside. He cares passionately about causes.

Never stuck for words, he is capable of talking endlessly. He is just as proficient at expressing himself through writing as talking.

Life's little luxuries and good living are appreciated. Despite a delicate digestion, he is fond of his food.

Spike's handwriting shows that he has green fingers. Gardening and the countryside would give him a feeling of peace and breathing space.

In livelier moments, foot-tapping rhythms, drama and theatre would exert a strong appeal.

Stephanie Beacham – Actress

Stephanie Beacham's erotic fantasies are mind-blowing. She wants and demands the best in sex, and is impatient with those who can't deliver. She is strongly rooted to the material and sensual.

This no-nonsense lady believes in getting down to the nitty-gritty. Foolish folk are cut down to size and once her mind is made up she rarely gets sidetracked.

At times her attitude is inflexible and unyielding as she far prefers arguing to get her own way than compromise.

Stephanie needs to be noticed. She sets about daily life with energy and is well-disciplined. Her rugged determination and forceful character make her click more comfortably with the male-type mind than with fluffy female scatterbrains. Her penetrating intellect can size up people and situations instantly.

Her handwriting shows a rebel who hates conformity. Those who choose the easy path through life are looked upon contemptuously.

Yet her cool and controlled responses curbing spontaneous displays of affection could be a bar to complete emotional happiness.

Much ado about
rien de tout —
very useful business
handwriting
much love
Stephanie

Stephanie Beacham

Neil Kinnock – Labour Party Leader

Hot-blooded, intense and passionate, Neil Kinnock, leader of the Labour Party, is ardent and demonstrative. He needs plenty of excitement.

He has to be loved and adored – and can be jealously possessive.

His temper is fiery. When pushed, he has to clench his fists to contain himself. But he is never at a loss for words, and speaking his mind gets things off his chest.

The flip side to his hot-headed and impetuous nature is a cold and calculating mind. Nothing can deter his determination. When his mind is fixed, he roars full-steam ahead, driven almost to the point of compulsion. He is always on the go.

Neil aspires to greatness and longs to hit the jackpot. Position and status are important to him.

At an everyday level, he likes to be listened to, but woe betide those who don't heed him.

He has a wicked sense of fun. Variety shows and unusual cabaret acts from belly-dancing to fire-eaters exert an appeal. If he were not a politician, he would relish the role of lion-tamer or ring-master, cracking the whip with a flourish to make others toe the line.

Although at an unconscious level he fears going to the edge and falling off, he knows that the chances are waiting for him, and he will eagerly grab them with both hands.

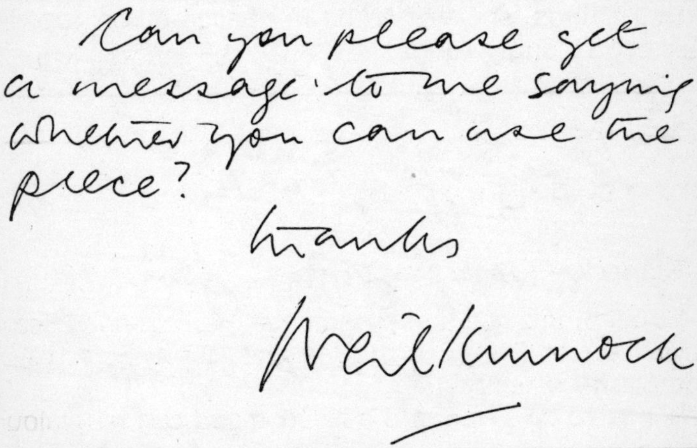
Can you please get a message to me saying whether you can use the piece?

thanks

Neil Kinnock

Neil Kinnock

Margaret Thatcher – Prime Minister

Beneath her well-tailored suits and brisk, business-like approach, Prime Minister Margaret Thatcher has a sensuousness and earthiness that even at 60 are attractive.

Her distinct writing shows she enjoys life's pleasures and values her comforts.

Frothiness, fussiness and elaboration bother her. She likes everything around her to be uncluttered and crystal-clear. That includes her emotional life. She was always more than capable of sorting the men from the boys.

Intuition and logic balance to make her judgement sharp and shrewd. She has a far-sighted, optimistic view of the future and her ambitious character, vitality and enthusiasm carry her ever onward and forward.

She knows how to take control forcefully and can lash out at those who are out of step. She knows what she wants and how to get it, firmly convinced her opinions and way are right.

In all things, she has to be in charge or on top. Her causes are strongly fought.

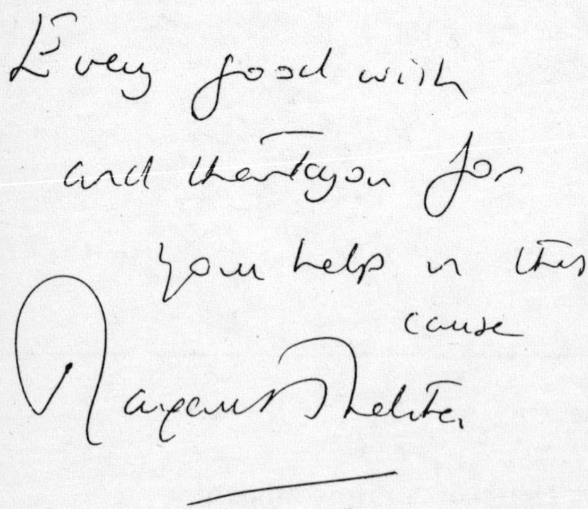

Margaret Thatcher

Well-planned, organized and with an impeccable sense of timing, her mind is agile and elastic and she stretches it to the full. Her wit is sharp. It helps her over many a hurdle, and her concentration and strategic mind overcome mental puzzles.

Yet there is a softer side to her character. She is loyal to those who support her, shielding lame ducks under her wing. Her appreciation of the arts would include a love of drama and a broad musical taste.

A perceptive imagination will always help her make her dreams come true.

Of further interest ...

WHAT YOUR HANDWRITING REVEALS

How to Master the Art of Graphology

- Do you have a natural sense of timing?
- Are you influenced by others?
- Do you have a visual conception of life?
- Are you extrovert or introvert?

You might think that only you can answer these questions - but this book shows that *anyone* who has seen your handwriting is able to expose your true character. Through the art of graphology - the interpretation of handwriting - your deepest secrets of personality, emotion, temperament - are revealed.

The techniques for analysing handwriting outlined in full detail in this book are now backed by scientific fact. Recent research into brain patterns has shown that our individual brain pattern, as well as our temperament and experience, will influence the flow of our writing.

Even the simplest word reveals something of our character - and therefore even the beginner can immediately start to make astounding discoveries about his own personality and that of others.

In this book **Margaret Gullan Whur** outlines all the techniques with step-by-step instructions so that you will soon be able to make your own interpretations.

SEXUAL PALMISTRY

The Intimate Revelations of Hand Analysis

What does the colour of your nails reveal about your sex drive? How can you distinguish an honest suitor from a dishonest one? Will he/she be faithful? Is this THE relationship? Whenever anyone visits a palmist the first questions they are likely to ask are about personal relationships – yet until now there has been no book which *solely* explores the extensive ramifications of a sexually orientated reading. **Nathaniel Altman** *here corrects that situation.* In this easy-to-read but remarkably detailed volume, he exposes – for anyone who can read the signs – the most intimate secrets of our psyche.

- Always choose the right man/woman
- Know if the relationship will be satisfactory – or not!
- Understand the hidden mysteries of your partner's mind...

with this, the first book *ever* to integrate scientific hand analysis with contemporary sexual psychology.